DATE DUE			

The Declaration of Independence

The Declaration of Independence

Other books in the At Issue in History series:

The Attack on Pearl Harbor
The Battle of Gettysburg
The Bill of Rights
The Conquest of the New World
The Crash of 1929
The Cuban Missile Crisis
Custer's Last Stand
The Discovery of the AIDS Virus
The Founding of the State of Israel
The Indian Reservation System
Japanese American Internment Camps
The McCarthy Hearings
The Nuremberg Trials
Reconstruction
The Rise of Adolf Hitler
The Salem Witch Trials
The Sinking of the Titanic
The Tiananmen Square Massacre
The Treaty of Versailles

The Declaration of Independence

Kelly Barth, *Book Editor*

AT ISSUE IN HISTORY

San Diego • Detroit • New York • San Francisco • Cleveland
New Haven, Conn. • Waterville, Maine • London • Munich

THOMSON
GALE

For more information, contact
Greenhaven Press
27500 Drake Rd.
Farmington Hills, MI 48331-3535
Or you can visit our Internet site at http://www.gale.com

Cover credit: © Hulton/Archive by Getty Images

Library of Congress, 14, 28
North Wind Picture Archives, 46, 96

LIBRARY OF CONGRESS CATALOGING-IN-PUBLICATION DATA

The Declaration of Independence / Kelly Barth, book editor.
p. cm. — (At issue in history)
Includes bibliographical references and index.
ISBN 0-7377-1576-6 (pbk. : alk. paper) — ISBN 0-7377-1575-8 (lib. : alk. paper)
1. United States. Declaration of Independence. 2. Civil rights—United States—History—Sources. 3. United States—Politics and government—Sources. I. Barth, Kelly. II. Series.
E221 .D29 2003
973.3'13—dc21 2002032212

Printed in the United States of America

Contents

Foreword

Historian Robert Weiss defines history simply as "a record and interpretation of past events." Both elements—record and interpretation—are necessary, Weiss argues.

> Names, dates, places, and events are the essence of history. But historical writing is not a compendium of facts. It consists of facts placed in a sequence to tell a connected story. A work of history is not merely a story, however. It also must analyze what happened and *why*—that is, it must interpret the past for the reader.

For example, the events of December 7, 1941, that led President Franklin D. Roosevelt to call it "a date which will live in infamy" are fairly well known and straightforward. A force of Japanese planes and submarines launched a torpedo and bombing attack on American military targets in Pearl Harbor, Hawaii. The surprise assault sank five battleships, disabled or sank fourteen additional ships, and left almost twenty-four hundred American soldiers and sailors dead. On the following day, the United States formally entered World War II when Congress declared war on Japan.

These facts and consequences were almost immediately communicated to the American people who heard reports about Pearl Harbor and President Roosevelt's response on the radio. All realized that this was an important and pivotal event in American and world history. Yet the news from Pearl Harbor raised many unanswered questions. Why did Japan decide to launch such an offensive? Why were the attackers so successful in catching America by surprise? What did the attack reveal about the two nations, their people, and their leadership? What were its causes, and what were its effects? Political leaders, academic historians, and students look to learn the basic facts of historical events and to read the intepretations of these events by many different sources, both primary and secondary, in order to develop a more complete picture of the event in a historical context.

In the case of Pearl Harbor, several important questions surrounding the event remain in dispute, most notably the role of President Roosevelt. Some historians have blamed his policies for deliberately provoking Japan to attack in order to propel America into World War II; a few have gone so far as to accuse him of knowing of the impending attack but not informing others. Other historians, examining the same event, have exonerated the president of such charges, arguing that the historical evidence does not support such a theory.

The Greenhaven At Issue in History series recognizes that many important historical events have been interpreted differently and in some cases remain shrouded in controversy. Each volume features a collection of articles that focus on a topic that has sparked controversy among eyewitnesses, contemporary observers, and historians. An introductory essay sets the stage for each topic by presenting background and context. Several chapters then examine different facets of the subject at hand with readings chosen for their diversity of opinion. Each selection is preceded by a summary of the author's main points and conclusions. A bibliography is included for those students interested in pursuing further research. An annotated table of contents and thorough index help readers to quickly locate material of interest. Taken together, the contents of each of the volumes in the Greenhaven At Issue in History series will help students become more discriminating and thoughtful readers of history.

Introduction

The Declaration of Independence was written in haste and copied onto common newsprint, belying its high purpose. Penned by Thomas Jefferson, the Declaration was the formal announcement to Britain and the world that the colonists intended to be free from British rule. After the American Revolution ended and a new framework of government was established, the Declaration was quickly swept off center stage. Over the years, the Declaration of Independence has been ignored and then rediscovered, disputed and defended, dismissed and pored over by scholars everywhere. Inspirational to some, threatening to others, its second paragraph in particular—declaring the freedom and equality of all people—has garnered much attention: "We hold these truths to be self-evident, that all men are created equal, that they are endowed by their Creator with certain inalienable rights, that among these are Life, Liberty, and the Pursuit of Happiness." Through the years since it was written, this passage has remained the most controversial statement contained in the document.

The Enlightenment Celebrated Rationality

The bold ideas Jefferson expressed in that second paragraph would not have surprised anyone familiar with the dominant philosophical movement of the time, the Enlightenment. America's principal proponent of Enlightenment thinking, Jefferson believed in an ordered universe in which all men could make use of their innate intelligence and reason to create a society of equals, one free of poverty and other social ills. Like other Enlightenment thinkers of the time, he believed that a divine creator had established a pattern of goodness that all people could instinctively follow. People, Jefferson believed, had an unlimited potential for intelligence and goodness and, as such, all deserved to be treated as free and equal to their fellow humans.

Another major component of Enlightenment thinking that influenced Jefferson was the idea that people could use a scientific approach to find answers to the most important questions in life. Following British philosophers such as David Hume and John Locke, Jefferson believed that in general, people behave in much the same way throughout time and around the world in response to an innate order. Jefferson used this rational approach to examine, among other topics, the intelligence and character of black slaves. He reported his findings in the document *Notes on the State of Virginia*, a book that served as an overall assessment of such things as his home state's environment, climate, and economic potential. After what he considered a thorough examination of his subjects, Jefferson found blacks inferior to whites in nearly every way. He said they were less intelligent, less handsome, and less able to make good moral choices.

Though in theory he agreed with the rest of the Enlightenment thinkers of his day that slavery was an abomination no matter what the skin color of the enslaved, Jefferson had serious misgivings about the practicality of freeing black slaves. He doubted their ability to take care of themselves, their families, or their properties if given the same freedom as whites.

Abolishing Slavery Was Easy Only in Theory

Even though in the Declaration of Independence he made the bold claim that all men are created equal and free, Jefferson's practical beliefs about, and his treatment of, blacks reveal that he did not completely believe what he had written. As historian John Chester Miller says of Jefferson in his book *Wolf by the Ears: Thomas Jefferson and Slavery*, "He enunciated American principles and ideas quite as though slavery and black Americans did not exist." In Jefferson's defense, Miller maintains that Jefferson truly believed that blacks were inferior and incapable of improving themselves beyond a certain level, which allowed him to tolerate the perpetuation of slavery. According to Miller, "Had [Jefferson] thought that he and his fellow Virginians were keeping in subjugation and debasement thousands of potential poets, philosophers, scientists, and men of letters . . . , he could not have endured even temporarily the continued existence of slavery." To his credit also, Jefferson had written a condemnation of slavery in his original draft of the Declaration of Independence, but the other colonists responsible for reviewing the draft, one-third of whom owned slaves themselves, edited it out. They wanted the document to declare their intention to protect their current way of life, not undermine it.

Throughout his political career, Jefferson continued to express the unpopular opinion that slavery should gradually be phased out of American life, but he personally did little to bring about this transition. In many scholars' minds, this has undercut the dramatic freedom-and-equality passage in the Declaration of Independence and weakened the credibility of Jefferson's argument that the institution of slavery should be dismantled. Miller continues, "While Jefferson regarded slavery as a 'hideous evil,' the bane of American society . . . , he was never able to cast aside the prejudices and fears which he had absorbed from his surroundings toward people of color; he did not free himself from his dependence on slave labor."

Rescued from Obscurity

In the fifteen or so years after it was written, Jefferson's Declaration of Independence was not, as would later be the case, quoted as a call for the end of slavery. People did not attribute more power to the equality passage than any other portion of the document. The Declaration of Independence was also not revered as it is today. In fact, it would have been difficult for the people of the time to regard with reverence a document that had been printed in pamphlet form and distributed by the thousands and mass-produced in newspapers. At the time the Declaration of Independence was written, people celebrated not the document declaring their independence but the Declaration itself. In fact, the Continental Congress's actual declaration of independence from Britain took place on July 2, 1776, while the Declaration of Independence was still being edited. It was only in later years that the observance of Independence Day took place on July 4, the day the document was actually signed, instead of July 2.

In the decade and a half during and after the Revolutionary War, the document was handled with anything but reverence. The original document had been written on cheap paper and was rolled up and hauled from battlefield to battlefield. After the war, it passed from hand to hand and moved from building to building. It became battered and badly faded.

In 1790, the Declaration of Independence was resurrected from this relative obscurity for political reasons and again became a central part of the national debate. The Republican Party began to focus on the document's second paragraph in particular as a statement of basic principles about government. They lauded the Declaration as a document that should guide all forming governments. In the process, they boasted about its writer, too; Jefferson was a member of their party rather than that of the opposing Federalists. On July 4, 1790, Republicans all over the country read the Declaration of Independence, and Republican-sponsored newspapers reprinted it. Federalists, however, did not join in the festivities. They thought that the document's free-and-equal language sounded too much like France's recent declaration, which had led to revolution and the massacre of the French monarchy. They also disliked it precisely because it had been written by Jefferson, a member of the opposition party.

After the War of 1812, the Federalist Party lost political power and dissolved, removing the last obstacle to the lauding of Jefferson and his most famous document. The parties remaining in power, the Whigs and the Jacksonians, claimed to descend both from the Republican Party and Jefferson and continued the rhetorical praise of the Declara-

Trumbull's famous painting depicts the signing of the Declaration of Independence on July 4, 1776.

tion unchallenged. At the same time, a fascination with the Revolutionary War and the founding of the country served to increase interest in the document. Biographies were written about the signers of the Declaration, and there was a new interest in finding and preserving the documents associated with the birth of the country.

Jefferson Encouraged Interest in the Declaration

Jefferson himself did much to promote interest in the document. As he aged, he came to rely on his reputation for having written the Declaration of Independence as being more important than anything else he had ever done. In fact, he planned that his tombstone would say, among few other things, that he was the author of the Declaration of American Independence. He took advantage of the rise in patriotic fervor to set in people's minds that his was a document of great import.

In fact, in 1817 when Congress commissioned muralist John Trumbull to paint four murals to hang in the Capitol, Jefferson suggested to Trumbull that one of them should portray the signing of the Declaration of Independence. Indeed, the twelve-foot-by-eighteen-foot canvas called *The Declaration of Independence* did become the most widely popular and most recognizable of the murals and did its part in reviving national interest in the document.

Both Jefferson and another important signer of the Declaration, John Adams, died on July 4, 1826, the fiftieth anniversary of the signing of the Declaration of Independence, which added to the mystique of the document. The two men were adulated and elevated, as was the document with which they had been so closely associated. In several well-reported eulogies of Jefferson, pastors continued to shift the focus off the document's statements about the Revolution and onto its passages about equality and freedom, calling them guiding principles of government.

A Guiding Principle of Government

At this point, the Declaration's transformation from a relatively unimportant historical footnote to one of history's most valued artifacts occurred. Instead of a document thought of primarily as a description of a people's commitment to overthrow an unjust regime, it became one that would be used to guide, limit, and shape the government it had helped in a small way to form. Though it was not a constitution or a bill of rights, documents normally used to shape governments and their legislation, the Declaration became a more widely familiar and obvious standard to which people expected the government to be accountable. Though not legally binding, the Declaration of Independence, especially the passage about freedom and equality, came to be viewed as morally binding.

Throughout the 1800s, politicians continued to argue over the meaning and implications of the Declaration's passage that all men are born free and equal. In their public senatorial debates, future president Abraham Lincoln and Stephen Douglas argued over what Jefferson had meant by these words. Douglas maintained that Jefferson was not referring to blacks when he used the term *men* in the Declaration of Independence. Lincoln would concede in these debates that all men, including black men, were not equal in every respect. But he maintained that the government must use the principles expressed in the Declaration of Independence to gradually phase out all institutions that contradicted its statement about freedom, equality, and opportunity for all people.

Others, such as Southern politician John C. Calhoun, did not, like Stephen Douglas, try to determine whom Jefferson had meant to protect in the second paragraph of the Declaration; instead, he flatly rejected the equality passage as simply wrong. Many political leaders shared Calhoun's fears that, given too much political clout, the Declaration of Independence's strong language about equality would obligate them to protect the rights of slaves, foreigners, women, and children.

These fears were justified. Throughout the 1800s, people across the country who had been dispossessed of their rights appealed to the nation's belief in the now familiar language of the second paragraph of the Declaration of Independence to secure these rights. Representatives from oppressed groups such as laborers, women, farmers, and blacks all began to call for changes in government policy that would more literally reflect their status as free and equal people. The most striking change brought about, in part, by the Declaration of Independence resulted because of Lincoln's and other abolitionists' belief that the Declaration's passage about the equality and freedom of all people demanded that the government put an end to slavery. This basic belief led the country into civil war and the eventual dismantling of the institution of slavery.

The Declaration of Independence is still quoted and discussed today. It is likely that people will continue to use the Declaration as a moral rallying cry to correct injustice.

Chapter 1

Thomas Jefferson and the Meaning of Equality

1

The Declaration Made Equality a Guiding Principle of Government

Pauline Maier

As historian Pauline Maier points out in the following passage from her book *American Scripture*, the Declaration of Independence was originally crafted to lead the American people to the threshold of revolution, to state a united determination to rebel against what many considered a tyrannical empire. Though Jefferson may have placed quite a different emphasis on the phrase "all men are created equal," by the time of his death in 1826, that phrase in particular had taken on much greater meaning. The eulogists at Jefferson's funeral called the native equality of all human beings one of the guiding principles of government, an idea that others began to believe as well. Though Jefferson had used such language to good effect as a defense of revolution against the British monarchy, he never intended it as a legally binding document. By elevating it to the status of a principle of government, these eulogists and many politicians to follow would place a heavy burden on the U.S. government, which would be increasingly bound to ensure that "all men" were protected under the law.

The right of revolution was not, it seems, the only "principle of liberty" in the Declaration of Independence, or even the most important for the guidance of posterity. "The same venerated instrument that declared our separation from Great Britain," said John Sergeant [a man who spoke

Pauline Maier, *American Scripture: Making the Declaration of Independence*, New York: Alfred A. Knopf, 1997.

on Jefferson and John Adams after their deaths] in Philadelphia, "contained also the memorable assertion, that 'all men are created equal, that they are endowed by their Creator with certain unalienable rights, and that to secure these rights, governments are instituted among men, deriving their just powers from the consent of the governed.'" And that, he said, "was the text of the revolution—the ruling vital principle—the hope that animated the patriot's heart and nerved the patriot's arm, when he looked forward through succeeding generations, and saw stamped upon all their institutions, the great principles set forth in the Declaration of Independence." For [Peleg] Sprague [who spoke on Jefferson and Adams at a ceremony after their deaths], too, the Declaration of Independence was a "Declaration, *by a whole people*, of what before existed, and will always exist, *the native equality of the human race*, as the true foundation of all political, of all human institutions."

Not only did its reference to men's equal creation concern people in a state of nature before government was established, but the document's original function was to end the previous regime, not to lay down principles to guide and limit its successor.

By including human equality among the "great principles" that the Declaration stated and describing it as "the foundation of all political, of all human institutions," Sergeant and Sprague contributed to a modern reading of the document that had begun to develop among Jeffersonian Republicans in the 1790s but became increasingly common after the 1820s, and gradually eclipsed altogether the document's assertion of the right of revolution. It is important to understand, however, that the issue of equality had a place in American life and politics long before it was associated with the Declaration of Independence. In the eighteenth century, the republican form of government was commonly considered best suited to egalitarian societies, and Americans, conscious that they lacked the extremes of wealth characteristic of older European countries, generally accepted equality as a characteristic of their society and of the governments they were founding. The state and local declarations of Independence made that abundantly clear. Remember that on May 15, 1776, the Virginia convention authorized the drafting of a new state constitution that would "secure substantial and equal liberty to the people." Two months earlier Judge William Henry Drayton praised South Carolina's new constitution for allowing voters to raise even the poorest Carolinian to the highest office in the state, while the Grand Jury at Charlestown took pleasure in the founding of a government whose benefits extended "generally, equally, and indiscriminately to all," and another grand jury in the Cheraws District took delight in the new constitution because under it "the rights and happiness of the whole, the poor and the rich, are equally secured." Meanwhile, Massachusetts coastal towns argued that the people's right to equal liberty and equal representation mandated a reallocation of legislative seats so they would be more closely keyed to population (which would, of course, shift power toward them). None of those references to equality had anything

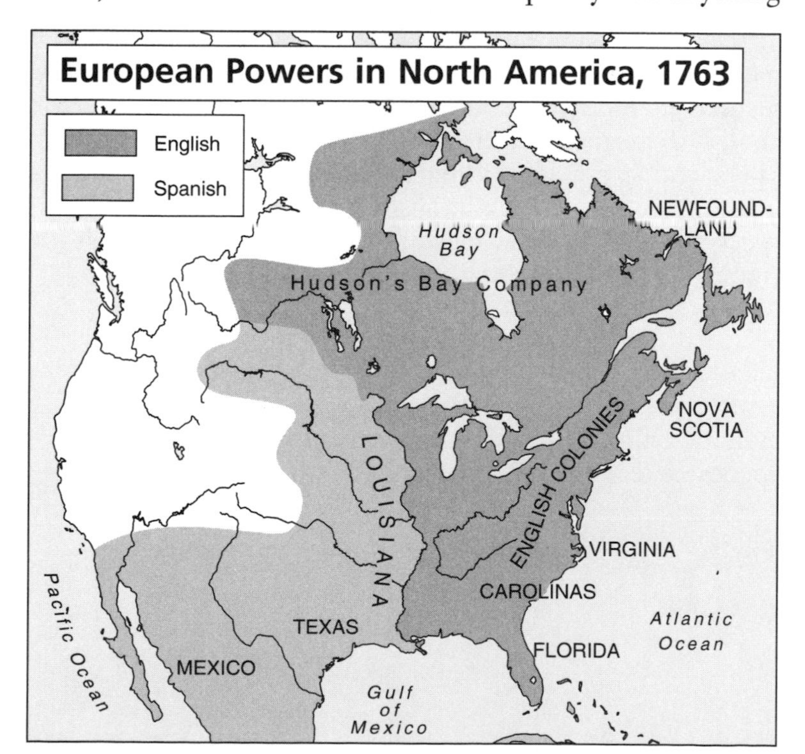

to do with the Declaration of Independence since they predated it. And together they suggested enough different meanings of the word "equality"—equal rights, equal access to office, equal voting power—to keep Americans busy sorting them out and fighting over practices that seemed inegalitarian far into the future. The equality mentioned, moreover, was generally between rich and poor white men, or those who lived in different geographical sections; its application to women or people of other races or persons with conflicting religious convictions would open whole new fields for conflict.

The Declaration Was Never Intended to Guide the Future Government

The Declaration of Independence was, in fact, a peculiar document to be cited by those who championed the cause of equality. Not only did its reference to men's equal creation concern people in a state of nature before government was established, but the document's original function was to end the previous regime, not to lay down principles to guide and limit its successor. True, the Declaration of Independence offered an implicit standard against which all governments could be compared and found wanting: unless they secured men's inalienable rights, the people could alter or abolish them and institute others "more likely to effect their safety and happiness." But the function of stating fundamental principles that established governments had to respect was normally entrusted to declarations or bills of rights like those attached to many state constitutions.

Jefferson's Words Were Not in Accord with His Life

Gregory Shafer

Thomas Jefferson, for all his fine words about freedom and equality in the Declaration of Independence, held some seemingly contradictory views about who in American society should have these freedoms. In the following article, writer and historian Gregory Shafer points out that Jefferson actually used the popular ideas of philosopher John Locke to defend his belief that only a few of the brightest and best white men should have the liberties spoken of in the Declaration. Shafer maintains that despite the veneration given him by his own and succeeding generations of Americans, Jefferson was at best an elitist, at worst a racist. As evidence he points out that Jefferson kept slaves until the end of his life and called the Native Americans foreigners who must either conform to the laws and customs of the encroaching white culture or face "extermination." In Jefferson's defense, Shafer points out that even today, while Americans boast of their egalitarian society, many government policies toward Native Americans, women, and homosexuals, for example, belie hypocrisy.

As we recall the words and deeds of the man perhaps most associated with American freedoms, we mustn't be ignorant of his unremitting campaign for the proliferation of slavery, his support of French oppression in Haiti, and his continuous subjugation of Native Americans. In-

Gregory Shafer, "Another Side of Thomas Jefferson," *The Humanist*, January/February 2002, pp. 16–20.

deed, while other national leaders of the time were emancipating their slaves and responding to the irrepressible thrusts of egalitarian rhetoric [political talk about equality], Thomas Jefferson was expanding his slave population and erecting special walls that secluded them from his majestic Monticello [Jefferson's home] in Virginia. In 1822—four years before his death—Jefferson's collection of slaves had risen to 267. Four years later, when he lay moribund, he found it proper only to free three, leaving the rest to languish in a nation that would grapple with the issue of forced servitude for another four decades.

David Walker, a prominent black Bostonian, was perhaps reacting to Jefferson's life of unabashed hypocrisy when in 1829 he warned African Americans that they should remember the third president as their greatest enemy. "Mr. Jefferson's remarks respecting us," Walker suggested, "have sunk deep into the hearts of millions of whites and will never be removed this side of eternity." In the end, what else could a former slave say about a man who championed freedom while proclaiming that "the amalgamation [blending] of whites with blacks produces a degradation to which no lover of his country, no lover of the excellence in the human character, can innocently consent."

To Understand Jefferson You Must Look at His Culture

Today, one cannot gaze upon the eloquent words or heroic deeds of Thomas Jefferson without also considering the more disquieting side of the man who has come to personify democracy, equality, and inalienable rights. Jefferson's legacy, his unflinching demand that government serve all the people, is forever tempered by his curious neglect and even disdain for those who didn't fit his lofty ideas for democracy. In many ways, then, Jefferson's life offers us a clear window into the experience of a great and ambitious man with profound weaknesses. . . . Perhaps we would do well to supplant our traditional deification with a judicious and realistic portrait of the man who lived to plant the seeds of freedom for his own social class while wrenching the roots away from others.

It isn't possible to extricate venerated men or women from the context in which they lived, and this is especially true of Thomas Jefferson. In a period when freedom was on the mind and lips of many, he was the quintessential progressive—the catalyst for revolutionary change in a time of tumult. In describing this ebullient young statesman, historian Gilbert Chinard, in *Thomas Jefferson: The Apostle of Americanism*, has suggested that Jefferson was the essence of enlightened thought, the consummate student of progressive thinkers in the path of [English philosopher] John Locke and [English statesman] Viscount Bolingbroke (Henry St. John).

> *Today, one cannot gaze upon the eloquent words or heroic deeds of Thomas Jefferson without also considering the more disquieting side of the man who has come to personify democracy, equality, and inalienable rights.*

When Jefferson joined other colonial representatives in Philadelphia for the crafting of the Declaration of Independence, he carried with him the authority of a large state and the cachet [indication of approval or status] of an intellectual who had studied Greek and Roman philosophers and listened to many of the day's great orators. To say that Jefferson was an Enlightenment intellectual is not only obvious but is helpful in understanding this complex man. Clearly he wasn't alone in his fervor to shape a new government and was hardly unique in his allusions to human rights advocates of the age. Jefferson had been raised on the eloquence of [American statesman] Patrick Henry and nurtured with learned instructors at the College of William and Mary. "The organized habit of criticism," which came to define the Age of Enlightenment, was firmly entrenched in Jefferson's psyche.

Indeed, reason and republicanism were bursting from various pockets of American thought. Throughout much of the land, radical ideas were flourishing, especially among the educated elite. For Jefferson and his colleagues it had become fashionable—even expected—to celebrate democracy and equality. As a new nation, many thought the United States would be unique in its embrace of unfettered human rights. As suggested by historian Gordon Wood in *The Creation of the American Republic*, there was a spirit of mission and purpose to create a land that was free and removed from ancient prejudice and privilege: "They told themselves over and over again that they were a numerous, sober, and industrious people, and therefore, as history showed, the ablest to contend with and the most successful in opposing tyranny." Wood believed "for Americans the future looked auspicious indeed." Little was impossible for a land comprised of rustic wisdom and youthful vivacity.

It was in this lofty scene that Thomas Jefferson lived and developed his philosophy. Rather than being a solitary philosopher in a barren land, Jefferson was one of many young thinkers who began to exult the words of John Locke and Jean Jacques Rousseau [French philosopher and writer], tailoring them to fit the goals of a new republic. Today, however, when people look to Jefferson as the catalyst or founder for quintessentially American ideals, they are only partially right. Jefferson's views, while democratic and inclusive, were also elitist and exclusive.

Rights Belonged Only to the Intelligent

From the prose of Locke, Jefferson embraced the notion that human rights were the right of all men who had the intellect to practice them effectively. Like Locke, Jefferson reserved the right to exclude those who were bereft of the requisite merit and acumen [mental power], and he was unabashed in his contempt for those who didn't meet his model of the man with natural rights. For Jefferson, rights were self-evident but only available to those who had the facility to detect and process them.

"Despite Locke's assertion that all men can have intuitive or self-evident perceptions, there is a potentially undemocratic element in this intuitive reason," writes historian Allen Jayne in *Jefferson's Declaration of Independence.* "What is self-evident to a highly educated and intelligent individual, seen clearly like bright sunshine, would often appear as darkness to an uneducated and unintelligent person." Therefore, in Jefferson's world, according to [historian] Morton White's *Philosophy of the American Revolution*, rights were limited to only a few highly intelligent and educated men. "The doctrine of self-evident truth could have been easily turned into a tool of haughty dictators of principles," says White. And Jayne adds, "Lockean self-evident epistemology [study of the nature of knowledge] established possibilities for an intellectual elite to exercise normative control over a democracy just as demonstrative reason did."

In short, freedom, equality, and undiluted emancipation weren't for average citizens but for those educated few who would lead the nation to greatness. Words such as merit were often bandied about and became the refuge of those—like Jefferson—who had ambivalent feelings about the rustic hoards which were coursing through the American bloodstream and adding color to its system. In writing about Jefferson's most enduring influences, Jayne acknowledges that "Locke's Second Treatise of Government made a profound influence on Jefferson," which is obvious "in the ideas expressed in the Declaration of Independence."

Minorities Had No Rights Because They Were Inferior

And so, as we chronicle the legacy of the man as it relates to those who were minorities in the United States and who failed to fit the mold of the enlightened individual, we begin to appreciate the tenets buttressing Jefferson's antipathy for African Americans, Native Americans, and those agrarians whom he often claimed to love. Because they were perceived as impervious to the natural reason used by educated patricians [persons of high birth and manners], they weren't part of the democratic experience. In many ways, Jefferson's view could be summarized by Matthew Arnold [English poet and critic], who would live and write a generation after Jefferson's death. Culture, wrote Arnold, doesn't have its origin in a curiosity but in the "love of perfection." For those who didn't have the ability to achieve a kind of intellectual and spiritual perfection, freedom was illusory. Such people simply didn't fit into Jefferson's paradigm [philosophical framework]. They weren't eligible. "Jefferson sought freedom for the people with whom he identified—a coalition of small-holders and gentlemen," notes Woody Holton in *Forced Founders*. Indians and slaves weren't meant to be independent but, rather, the "fruits of independence."

Historian Howard Zinn recalls a particularly humorous event that perhaps best epitomizes the kind of selective and limited concept of human rights held by Jefferson and many of the founders. During those heady days of the [second president] John Adams administration, when various leaders had gathered in the House of Representatives, a fight took place between two congressional representatives. According to Zinn in *Declarations of Independence*, Matthew Lyon of Vermont spat on Roger Griswold of Connecticut as the two fought over an unknown issue. Later, after the two had been separated, a Bostonian wrote angrily of Lyon, "I feel grieved that the saliva of an Irishman should be left upon the face of an American." Earlier, it is revealing to note, Lyon had written an article deriding the Adams administration as filled with "power and an unbounded thirst for ridiculous pomp, foolish adulation, and selfish avarice." For his political convictions, Lyon was tried and found guilty under the Sedition Act [legislation governing acts of political rebellion] and imprisoned for four months.

Thomas Jefferson

From such an elitist view, it was easy for Jefferson to see those of African descent—either from the United States or elsewhere in the hemisphere—as little more than property for exploitation and enslavement. For example, prior to the American Revolution, when the British under the colonial governor of Virginia, Lord John Murray Dunmore, sought in 1774 to use blacks as soldiers to quell a rebellion, Jefferson was one of many who began a vehement argument opposing Dunmore on behalf of slave-owners and their fear of a collective uprising.

The More Freedom Slaves Had the More Dangerous They Became

Later, Jefferson wrote angrily in response to the governor's call for slave emancipation, suggesting, according to Holton, that "Dunmore's emancipation proclamation was a major cause of the American Revolution." Consequently, during much of the revolution, Jefferson and other founding fathers were busy trying to stifle the liberation of slaves and protect the rights of their masters. "Slaves had always resisted their condition," concludes Holton in discussing the uprising during the days of the revolution. "In 1774 they began conspiring to exploit the opportunities presented them by the imperial crisis." It was Jefferson and his colleagues, then, who found themselves in the rather dubious position of combating the liberation of a manifestly oppressed group—a clear indication of how narrow was the extent of Jefferson's philosophy.

Even during the revolution, Jefferson was quick to contradict the contentions of Alexander Hamilton when the latter suggested that slaves should be recruited as soldiers. In Jefferson's view, their participation would only spoil them as docile workers by teaching them how to fight and by opening their eyes to the possibilities of freedom and the dream of emancipation. This might lead to slave insurrections later. Furthermore, Jefferson saw blacks as inherently inferior, unable to even comprehend the precarious situation to which they were being exposed. "While admitting that they sometimes displayed courage, he attributed their valor to their inability to fully appreciate the peril in which their actions took them," writes John Chester Miller in *The Wolf by the Ears: Thomas Jefferson and Slavery*. To add insult to injury, Jefferson later approved a bill that rewarded all white men who fought in the Revolution with 300 acres of land and a healthy black slave.

From such an elitist view, it was easy for Jefferson to see those of African descent—either from the United States or elsewhere in the hemisphere—as little more than property for exploitation and enslavement.

When Jefferson ascended to the presidency in 1801, he was faced with the reality of the Haitian republic under black revolutionary Francois Toussaint. At that time, [French leader] Napoleon Bonaparte began moving ships to Haiti to regain control of the former French colony. So Jefferson made it clear that he personally had no love for "this black republic" and that the United States would support Napoleon. According to historian Conor Cruise O'Brien in *The Long Affair: Thomas Jefferson and the French Revolution, 1785–1800*, Jefferson indicated that, if Napoleon could simply make peace with England, "then nothing will be easier than to furnish your army and fleet with everything, and reduce Toussaint to starvation."

Applying these sentiments, Jefferson reversed the policy embraced by presidents Adams and Washington and encouraged Napoleon to attack and try to recolonize Haiti. Roger Kennedy, in *Orders from France: The Americans and the French in a Revolutionary World, 1780–1820*, confirms that the previous federalist administrations had secured arms and food for Toussaint, but now Jefferson's Democratic Republican administration proceeded to loan France $300,000 "for relief of whites on the island." Hence, according to Kennedy, in Jefferson's eyes "a Napoleonic colony was to be preferred to a Negro republic in the West Indies, especially when France intended the reimposition of slavery and, thus, some alleviation of the fears of the slave owners" in the southern United States. When Napoleon's efforts failed, Jefferson still refused to acknowledge Haiti as a sovereign state.

In the United States, though slavery was an ensconced institution, it was clear that many citizens didn't embrace it. Also, Washington and other of the nation's founders (at least at the time of their deaths) liberated their slaves. Jefferson, however, not only compelled their continued servitude but, during his presidency, created legislation to make their lives more amenable to their southern masters. Slavery was never an issue that Jefferson wanted to resolve through integration or emancipation. Rather, his plan was to ship slaves to a colony of their own in the West Indies, to dispose of them as people unable to coexist with their white counterparts, or to simply eliminate them through forced removal. "Jefferson's slaveholding," writes [historian] Richard Lowen in *Lies My Teacher Told Me*, "affected almost everything he did, from his opposition to internal improvements to his foreign policy. By 1820, Jefferson had become an ardent advocate of the expansion of slavery to the Western territories."

Jefferson Considered Native Americans Foreign

Regarding Native Americans, Jefferson's philosophy was a confluence [mixture] of contempt and condescension. He was fond of lecturing about the novelties of the native language and culture but only in the most elitist manner. For much of his life, Jefferson perceived natives as foreigners in a land that was destined to be part of a great white empire, and his policies—both overtly and more surreptitiously—were crafted to dispossess them of their homes. "The Jeffersonian vision of the destiny of the Americas," writes [historian] Anthony Wallace in *Jefferson and the Indians*, "had no place for Indians as Indians. In Jefferson's view, the Indian nations would be either civilized and incorporated into mainstream American society or, failing this . . . exterminated."

Could it be that Jefferson, with all of his lofty theories and inconsistent actions, truly does epitomize that which is best and worst in our national persona?

During the early years of his adult life, Jefferson worked assiduously to wrest native lands away from various tribes. With western property representing a lucrative windfall for those who obtained it, he was one of dozens who sought patents from the British Empire for land west of the Appalachian Mountains. With little concern for native autonomy or the injustice of usurping land for profit, Jefferson and other Virginia gentlemen lobbied British officials to open the land to patents. And when British officials declined, citing the trouble and expense a protracted war with various tribes would cause, Jefferson and others were quick to make the opening of new land a patriotic issue, claiming that the failure of the English to assist them in taking native property was tantamount to oppression. This claim, as Holton suggests throughout his book, was an impetus for the gradual fissure dividing the British from the colonists. Instead of only being about taxation and representation, the American Revolution had much to do with annexing new land for white settlements and profits that would follow.

In the 1760s, Kentucky was the principal hunting ground for a variety of native tribes, and it was critical for their future survival that they maintain these grounds and remain free from continued white incursion. Indeed, earlier treaties between the tribes and the British had been consummated with the understanding that native land would be respected if natives ceased to wage war on colonists. The problem—

at least from Jefferson's perspective—was that Kentucky and other western lands were being settled by the flood of new immigrants who saw the opportunity for new land as a chance for a new life. Settlers meant profits for Jefferson and his partners if they could only win patents for the land from the English government or by stealing it.

So, in the early years before the revolution, Jefferson and other venerated Americans were busy trying to reverse the promised policy of the British and open the lands for their collective avarice. According to Wallace, Jefferson made attempts to acquire "a total of about 35,000 acres." More revealing for our examination, when he became president and was confronted with violations of the treaty by white settlers who were living on native land, Jefferson took "measures to ensure that their encroachments on Cherokee land would be legitimized by appropriate land cession."

Americans Still Judge Who Deserves Liberty

With such an unseemly record, one wonders why Thomas Jefferson has become such an American icon in the centuries following his life. While our third president was a person of exulted ruminations about the republic he and his colleagues were creating, he joins other founding fathers in their general distrust and antipathy for those who were non-European—for those who didn't fit their paradigm of a person who deserved liberty and justice. In doing this it's important to remember that Jefferson was hardly different from others of his time, and his actions were, in many ways, the harbinger [foreshadower of a future event] of a national policy that would continue through the present day.

For no matter how much we would like to wring our hands or deride Jefferson's hypocrisy, we must acknowledge our own provincial policies in the twenty-first century—policies that have the same parochial stamp as Jefferson's. Two hundred fifty years ago the policy was punitive against people outside the established mainstream. Today, in our more enlightened age, we see scant movement on a law to extend the basic right to marry to gays and lesbians. In the Roman Catholic and Southern Baptist churches we see equally little evidence that women are being treated as equals. And in our concomitant [accompanying] policy toward Native Americans, there is a lamentable failure to reverse the alcoholism and abject poverty that runs rampant through their communities and is a direct result of the founding principles of the United States.

Could it be that Jefferson, with all of his lofty theories and inconsistent actions, truly does epitomize that which is best and worst in our national persona? Could it be that the complete Jefferson—replete with the blemishes of racism and genocide—more accurately personifies his country centuries after his death? For while we aspire to the apogee of democratic values—always elevating the United States above those who are less free or egalitarian—we seem willing to ignore those who don't meet our time-honored image of citizen. "Since Thomas Jefferson did more than any other founding father to shape and articulate the ideas and ideals upon which American civilization is based, it seems logical to judge him by the positive or negative impact of those ideas and ideals," writes Jayne.

To that suggestion, I agree. Jefferson, with all of his flaws and indiscretions, is the quintessential American. And like other great leaders of this republic, he accomplished much while clearly being a product—and victim—of his age.

Blacks Are Inferior to Whites

Thomas Jefferson

Thomas Jefferson adhered to the philosophical tradition of his time, the Enlightenment, believing that all things in life could best be explained in rational, scientific terms. In the following passage about blacks from his 1787 book *Notes on the State of Virginia*, Jefferson cites his own dispassionate observations of blacks as evidence to demonstrate their basic inferiority to whites and even to Native Americans. He relies on his readers' agreement with his basic assumptions about standards of beauty, artistic talent, and normal behavior. Though Jefferson would be lauded for his statement in the Declaration of Independence about the equality of all men, this passage demonstrates that he believed blacks could not be measured by the same standard as other men and thus could not be extended the same kinds of freedoms and responsibilities.

The first difference which strikes us is that of colour. Whether the black of the negro resides in the reticular membrane between the skin and scarf-skin, or in the scarf-skin itself; whether it proceeds from the colour of the blood, the colour of the bile, or from that of some other secretion, the difference is fixed in nature, and is as real as if its seat and cause were better known to us. And is this difference of no importance? Is it not the foundation of a greater or less share of beauty in the two races? Are not the fine mixtures of red and white, the expressions of every passion by greater or less suffusions of colour in the one, preferable to that

Thomas Jefferson, *Notes on the State of Virginia*, London: Stockdale, 1787.

eternal monotony, which reigns in the countenances, that immoveable veil of black which covers all the emotions of the other race? Add to these, flowing hair, a more elegant symmetry of form, their own judgment in favour of the whites, declared by their preference of them, as uniformly as is the preference of the Oranootan [orangutan] for the black women over those of his own species. The circumstance of superior beauty, is thought worthy attention in the propagation of our horses, dogs, and other domestic animals; why not in that of man? Besides those of colour, figure, and hair, there are other physical distinctions proving a difference of race. They have less hair on the face and body.

The circumstance of superior beauty, is thought worthy attention in the propagation of our horses, dogs, and other domestic animals; why not in that of man?

They secrete less by the kidnies, and more by the glands of the skin, which gives them a very strong and disagreeable odour. This greater degree of transpiration renders them more tolerant of heat, and less so of cold, than the whites. Perhaps too a difference of structure in the pulmonary apparatus, which a late ingenious experimentalist has discovered to be the principal regulator of animal heat, may have disabled them from extricating, in the act of inspiration, so much of that fluid from the outer air, or obliged them in expiration, to part with more of it. They seem to require less sleep. A black, after hard labour through the day, will be induced by the slightest amusements to sit up till midnight, or later, though knowing he must be out with the first dawn of the morning. They are at least as brave, and more adventuresome. But this may perhaps proceed from a want of fore-thought, which prevents their seeing a danger till it be present. When present, they do not go through it with more coolness or steadiness than the whites. They are more ardent after their female: but love seems with them to be more an eager desire, than a tender delicate mixture of sentiment and sensation. Their griefs are transient. Those numberless afflictions, which render it doubtful whether heaven has given life to us in mercy or in wrath, are less felt, and sooner forgotten with them. In general, their existence appears to participate more of sensation than reflection. To this must be ascribed their disposition to sleep when abstracted from their diversions, and unemployed in labour. An animal whose body is at rest, and who does not reflect, must be disposed to sleep of course. Comparing them by their faculties of memory, reason, and imagination, it appears to me, that in memory they are equal to the whites; in reason much inferior, as I think one could scarcely be found capable of tracing and comprehending the investigations of Euclid; and that in imagination they are dull, tasteless, and anomalous. It would be unfair to follow them to Africa for this investigation. We will consider them here, on the same stage with the whites, and where the facts are not apocryphal on which a judgment is to be formed. It will be right to make great allowances for the difference of condition, of education, of conversation, of the sphere in which they move. Many millions of them have been brought to, and born in America. Most of them indeed have been confined to tillage, to their own homes, and their own society: yet many have been so situated, that they might have availed themselves of the conversation of their masters; many have been brought up to the handicraft arts, from that circumstance have always been associated with the whites. Some have been liberally educated, and all have lived in countries where the arts and sciences are cultivated to a considerable degree, and have had before their eyes samples of the best works from abroad. The Indians, with no advantages of this kind, will often carve figures on their pipes not destitute of design and merit. They will crayon out an animal, a plant, or a country, so as to prove the existence of a germ in their minds which only wants cultivation. They astonish you with strokes of the most sublime oratory; such as prove their reason and sentiment strong, their imagination glowing and elevated. But never yet could I find that a black had uttered a thought above the level of plain narration; never see even an elementary trait of painting or sculpture. In music they are more generally gifted than the whites with accurate ears for tune and time, and they have been found capable of imagining a small catch [a round for three or more voices, usually male]. Whether they will be equal to the composition of a more extensive run of melody, or of complicated harmony, is yet to be proved. Misery is often the parent of the most affecting touches in poetry.—Among the blacks is misery enough, God knows, but no poetry. Love is the peculiar cestrum of the poet. Their love is ardent, but it kindles the senses only, not the imagination. Religion indeed has produced a Phyllis Whately [Phyllis Wheatley, eighteenth-century black American poet]; but it could not produce a poet. The compositions published under her name are below the dignity of criticism. . . . Ignatius Sancho [a black British writer] has approached nearer to merit in composition; yet his letters do more honour to the heart than the head. They breathe the purest effusions of friendship and general philanthropy, and shew how great a degree of the latter may be compounded with strong religious zeal. He is often happy in the turn of his compliments, and his style is easy and familiar. . . . But his imagination is wild and extravagant, escapes incessantly from every restraint of reason and taste, and, in the course of its vagaries, leaves a tract of thought as incoherent and eccentric, as is the course of a meteor through the sky. His subjects should often have led him to a process of sober reasoning: yet we find him always substituting sentiment for demonstration. Upon the whole, though we admit him to the first place among those of his own colour who have presented themselves to the public judgment, yet when we compare him with the writers of the race among whom he lived, and particularly with the epistolary class, in which he has taken his own stand, we are compelled to enroll him at the bottom of the column. This criticism supposes the letters published under his name to be genuine, and to have received amendment from no other hand; points which would not be of easy investigation. The improvement of the blacks in body and mind, in the first instance of their mixture with the whites, has been observed by every one, and proves that their inferiority is not the effect merely of their condition of life.

The Declaration and the Problem of Slavery

1
Jefferson Should Work to Abolish Slavery

Benjamin Banneker

In 1792, scientist and Maryland free Negro Benjamin Banneker sent Secretary of State Thomas Jefferson the manuscripts of his *Almanac*, a publication containing astrological and meteorological data for a given year. That was not, however, the only thing he sent. In the following cover letter that accompanied the manuscript, Banneker appeals to Jefferson's belief in the basic equality of all humans as expressed in the Declaration of Independence, and urges him to use his political position to secure the freedom of black slaves. He also reminds Jefferson that just as he and his comrades fought the Revolutionary War to secure respect and fair treatment from the British, Banneker and his fellow blacks desired and deserved the same treatment from whites. Banneker's almanac and the wisdom and intelligence he displayed in the letter so impressed Jefferson that he sent the *Almanac* to the Academy of Sciences in Paris.

To Thomas Jefferson

I am fully sensible of that freedom, which I take with you in the present occasion; a liberty which seemed to me scarcely allowable, when I reflected on that distinguished and dignified station in which you stand, and the almost general prejudice and prepossession, which is so prevalent in the world against those of my complexion.

I suppose it is a truth too well attested to you, to need a proof here, that we are a race of beings, who have long la-

Benjamin Banneker, letter to Thomas Jefferson, Philadelphia, 1792.

bored under the abuse and censure of the world; that we have long been looked upon with an eye of contempt; and that we have long been considered rather as brutish than human, and scarcely capable of mental endowments.

Sir, I hope I may safely admit, in consequence of that report which hath reached me, that you are a man less inflexible in sentiments of this nature, than many others; that you are measurably friendly, and well disposed towards us; and that you are willing and ready to lend your aid and assistance to our relief, from those many distresses, and numerous calamities, to which we are reduced.

All Are Given the Same Faculties by God

Now Sir, if this is founded in truth, I apprehend you will embrace every opportunity, to eradicate that train of absurd and false ideas and opinions, which so generally prevails with respect to us; and that your sentiments are concurrent with mine, which are, that one universal Father hath given being to us all; and that he hath not only made us all of one flesh, but that he hath also, without partiality, afforded us all the same sensations and endowed us all with the same faculties; and that however variable we may be in society or religion, however diversified in situation or color, we are all in the same family and stand in the same relation to him.

I apprehend you will embrace every opportunity, to eradicate that train of absurd and false ideas and opinions, which so generally prevails with respect to us; and that your sentiments are concurrent with mine, which are, that one universal Father hath given being to us all.

Sir, if these are sentiments of which you are fully persuaded, I hope you cannot but acknowledge, that it is the indispensable duty of those, who maintain for themselves the rights of human nature, and who possess the obligations of Christianity, to extend their power and influence to the relief of every part of the human race, from whatever burden or oppression they may unjustly labor under; and this, I apprehend, a full conviction of the truth and obligation of these principles should lead all to.

Sir, I have long been convinced, that if your love for yourselves, and for those inestimable laws, which preserved to you the rights of human nature, was founded on sincerity, you could not but be solicitous [giving what is asked], that every individual, of whatever rank or distinction, might with you equally enjoy the blessings thereof; neither could you rest satisfied short of the most active effusion [unrestrained expression] of your exertions, in order to the promotion from any state of degradation, to which the unjustifiable cruelty and barbarism of men may have reduced them.

Sir, I freely and cheerfully acknowledge, that I am of the African race, and in that color which is natural to them of the deepest dye; and it is under a sense of the most profound gratitude to the Supreme Ruler of the Universe, that I now confess to you, that I am not under that state of tyrannical thraldom [a state of servitude], and inhuman captivity, to which too many of my brethren are doomed, but that I have abundantly tasted of the fruition of those blessings, which proceed from that free and unequalled liberty with which you are favored; and which, I hope, you will willingly allow you have mercifully received, from the immediate hand of that Being, from whom proceedeth every good and perfect Gift.

The Revolution Was Fought to Secure Liberty

Sir, suffer me to recall to your mind that time, in which the arms and tyranny of the British crown were exerted, with every powerful effort, in order to reduce you to a state of servitude: look back, I entreat you, on the variety of dangers to which you were exposed; reflect on that time, in which every human aid appeared unavailable, and in which even hope and fortitude wore the aspect of inability to the conflict, and you cannot but be led to a serious and grateful sense of your miraculous and providential preservation; you cannot but acknowledge, that the present freedom and tranquility which you enjoy you have mercifully received, and that it is the peculiar blessing of Heaven.

This, Sir, was a time when you clearly saw into the injustice of a state of slavery, and in which you had just apprehensions of the horror of its condition. It was now that your abhorrence [extreme rejection] thereof was so excited, that you publicly held forth this true and invaluable doctrine, which is worthy to be recorded and remembered in all succeeding ages: 'We hold these truths to be self-evident, that all men are created equal; that they are endowed by their Creator with certain unalienable rights, and that among these are, life, liberty, and the pursuit of happiness.'

Blacks Should Have Liberty as Well

Here was a time, in which your tender feelings for yourselves had engaged you thus to declare, you were then impressed with proper ideas of the great violation of liberty, and the free possession of those blessings, to which you were entitled by nature; but, Sir, how pitiable is it to reflect, that although you were so fully convinced of the benevolence of the Father of Mankind, and of his equal and impartial distribution of these rights and privileges, which he hath conferred upon them, that you should at the same time counteract his mercies, in detaining by fraud and violence so numerous a part of my brethren, under groaning captivity, and cruel oppression, that you should at the same time be found guilty of that most criminal act, which you professedly detested in others, with respect to yourselves.

I suppose that your knowledge of the situation of my brethren, is too extensive to need a recital here; neither shall I presume to prescribe [suggest] methods by which they may be relieved, otherwise than by recommending to you and all others, to wean yourselves from those narrow prejudices which you have imbibed [taken in] with respect to them, and as Job proposed to his friends, 'put your soul in their souls' stead'; thus shall your hearts be enlarged with kindness and benevolence towards them; and thus shall you need neither the direction of myself or others, in what manner to proceed herein.

And now, Sir, although my sympathy and affection for my brethren hath caused my enlargement thus far, I ardently hope, that your candor and generosity will plead with you in my behalf, when I make known to you, that it was not originally my design; but having taken up my pen in order to direct to you, as a present, a copy of my Almanac, which I have calculated for the succeeding year, I was unexpectedly and unavoidably led thereto.

This calculation is the product of my arduous study, in this most advanced stage of life; for having long had unbounded desires to become acquainted with the secrets of nature, I have had to gratify my curiosity herein through my own assiduous [careful and persistent] application to Astronomical Study, in which I need not recount to you the many difficulties and disadvantages which I have had to encounter.

And although I had almost declined to make my calculation for the ensuing year, in consequence of that time which I had allotted therefor, being taken up at the Federal Territory. . . yet finding myself under several engagements to Printers of this State, to whom I had communicated my design, on my return to my place of residence, I industriously applied myself thereto, which I hope I have accomplished with correctness and accuracy; a copy of which I have taken the liberty to direct to you, and which I humbly request you will favorably receive; and although you may have the opportunity of perusing it after its publication; yet I choose to send it to you in manuscript previous thereto, that thereby you might not only have an earlier inspection, but that you might also view it in my own hand writing.

Slavery Is Incompatible with the Declaration of Independence

William Lloyd Garrison

For William Lloyd Garrison, the Declaration of Independence represented more than just a statement of rights of oppressed colonists; it was also a call to overturn a government that violated the rights of any people. Garrison was a leader of one of the more radical groups of abolitionists, an antislavery group that gained in fervor in the decades just before the Civil War. He referred to the Declaration of Independence more than any other political document to point out that the freedom of every American was guaranteed, regardless of race. Not surprisingly, he and his fellow abolitionists called upon the Declaration of Independence at public meetings, such as the one described in the following letter to defend their idea that it would be necessary to dissolve the Union if it continued to support a government that made it legal to enslave other humans.

To *The Liberator*

New-York, [May] 11, 1847.

My Dear Friend:

Our anniversary meeting [American Anti-Slavery Society] has just closed. It was attended by a large throng of highly intelligent and reflecting persons, and the proceedings were of the most satisfactory and inspiring character. I am satisfied that an unusually powerful impression was made on the minds of those present. The attention they

William Lloyd Garrison, "Garrison to *The Liberator*," *The Liberator*, May 14, 1847.

gave to the various speakers was deep and earnest, and they frequently responded in bursts of enthusiastic approval to the bold and stirring sentiments that were uttered. Occasionally, a few hisses could be heard from some evil spirits who were tormented just at the right time, but their opposition was very feeble, and only served to bring out all the better feelings of the audience in loud and protracted applause. The result has clearly demonstrated a wonderful change in public sentiment, especially in this city, within a comparatively short period. To-day, on our platform, doctrines were maintained, and sentiments advanced, in regard to Church and State, the Union and the Constitution, not only without uproar, but with strong approval, that would have subjected us to great peril, if they had been uttered a few years since. As sure as the sun shines, or water rolls, or the grass is growing, our anti-slavery leaven is fermenting the whole lump of society. God is with us, and never working more diligently for us, than when the clouds are the thickest, and the prospect most dubious. At the commencement of the meeting, I read [from the Bible] portions of the 2d and 18th chapters of Jeremiah, which seemed to me singularly applicable to the history and career of this country—its deliverance from colonial vassalage [submission to a political power], its subsequent forgetfulness of God, its grievous wandering from the path of justice, its worship of the Moloch [a god to whom children were sacrificed] of slavery, its liability to divine retribution. Our beloved and unswerving friend Samuel May, Jr., formerly of Leicester, but now of Brooklyn, Ct., followed in a devout and earnest prayer for guidance, strength, and victory over the dark spirit of oppression. . . . Wendell Phillips then offered the following resolution:

Slavery Must End Despite Fear of Conflict

Resolved, That the duty of every American is to give his sympathy and aid to the anti-slavery movement; and the first duty of every citizen is to devote himself to the destruction of the Union and the Constitution, which have already shipwrecked the experiment of civil liberty, and bid fair to swallow up the hopes of every honest man in a worse than military despotism; assured that out of the wreck, we may confidently expect a State which will unfold, in noble proportions, the principles of the Declaration of Independence, whose promises made us once the admiration of the world.

This resolution was advocated by Mr. Phillips with that earnestness, boldness and eloquence, which mark him as the James Otis [American Revolution leader] of the new revolution for liberty. It had many passages of great power, which went through the vast assembly with electric effect.

William Lloyd Garrison

The platform was next taken by Frederick Douglass . . . The following is the resolution which was sustained by Douglass:

Resolved, That slavery is a system so demoralizing and inhuman, so impious and atheistical, so hostile to the cause of liberty and Christianity throughout the world, that to seek its immediate extinction in this and every other country where it is tolerated, is the right and the duty of the people of all nations, by all proper instrumentalities:—That this Society, as the representative of three millions of American slaves, proffers its grateful acknowledgments to the Christians and philanthropists of England, Scotland, Ireland and Wales, for the powerful testimonies that they have borne against the sin of slaveholding, under all circumstances, and especially in a land boasting of its civil and religious liberty—for their warm approval of the anti-slavery movement in the United States, and those who are its unflinching advocates—and for the charitable aid they have extended to us, in various ways, from time to time; assuring them that they have neither labored nor spoken in vain, and invoking them to continue their co-operative efforts, until the last slave on the American soil is set free.

Douglass was eminently successful in his speech, and was warmly applauded from beginning to end.

The meeting began at 10, and terminated at 1 o'clock, on the topmost wave of popular gratification. I regret that our stanch friend from the West, James W. Walker, had no opportunity, for lack of time, to address the assembly, but he will speak this evening at the Apollo Saloon. We have quite a number of our truest friends brought together from various parts of the country, and I have no doubt our subsequent meetings will be highly interesting and edifying.

To-morrow evening, our colored friends in this city will give Douglass a grand reception meeting.

In haste, but with renovated spirit,

Faithfully yours,

WM. LLOYD GARRISON.

All Men Are Not Created Equal

John C. Calhoun

Southern statesman John C. Calhoun was so dismayed by what he saw as a political movement toward considering blacks equal to whites that he wrote the following passage in his pamphlet, *A Disquisition on Government*. He places direct blame for this erroneous thinking on the "all men are created equal" wording in the Declaration of Independence. In this passage, he attempts to dismantle the underpinnings of Jefferson's beliefs about equality. Calhoun says that though Jefferson assumed people were equal in "the state of nature," or before laws or organized societies existed, there never really was such a time. He maintains that people have always lived in association with each other and that, of necessity, has meant that those with stronger mental, physical, and moral character must have more freedom and power than their inferiors. Calhoun maintains that blacks, as inferior people, neither deserve complete freedom nor would be capable of governing their own behavior should it be given to them.

To perfect society, it is necessary to develope the faculties, intellectual and moral, with which man is endowed. But the main spring to their development, and, through this, to progress, improvement and civilization, with all their blessings, is the desire of individuals to better their condition. For, this purpose, liberty and security are indispensable. Liberty leaves each free to pursue the course he may deem best to promote his interest and happiness, as

John C. Calhoun, *A Disquisition on Government*, published by John C. Calhoun, 1853.

far as it may be compatible with the primary end for which government is ordained;—while security gives assurance to each, that he shall not be deprived of the fruits of his exertions to better his condition. These combined, give to this desire the strongest impulse of which it is susceptible. For, to extend liberty beyond the limits assigned, would be to weaken the government and to render it incompetent to fulfil its primary end,—the protection of society against dangers, internal and external. The effect of this would be, insecurity; and, of insecurity,—to weaken the impulse of individuals to better their condition, and thereby retard progress and improvement. On the other hand, to extend the powers of the government, so as to contract the sphere assigned to liberty, would have the same effect, by disabling individuals in their efforts to better their condition.

But some communities require a far greater amount of power than others to protect them against anarchy and external dangers.

Herein is to be found the principle which assigns to power and liberty their proper spheres, and reconciles each to the other under all circumstances. For, if power be necessary to secure to liberty the fruits of its exertions, liberty, in turn, repays power with interest, by increased population, wealth, and other advantages, which progress and improvement bestow on the community. By thus assigning to each its appropriate sphere, all conflicts between them cease; and each is made to co-operate with and assist the other, in fulfilling the great ends for which government is ordained.

Amounts of Freedom and Power Should Vary

But the principle, applied to different communities, will assign to them different limits. It will assign a larger sphere to power and a more contracted one to liberty, or the reverse, according to circumstances. To the former, there must ever be allotted, under all circumstances, a sphere sufficiently large to protect the community against danger from without and violence and anarchy within. The residuum [what remains] belongs to liberty. More cannot be safely or rightly allotted to it.

But some communities require a far greater amount of

power than others to protect them against anarchy and external dangers; and, of course, the sphere of liberty in such, must be proportionally contracted. The causes calculated to enlarge the one and contract the other, are numerous and various. Some are physical;—such as open and exposed frontiers, surrounded by powerful and hostile neighbors. Others are moral;—such as the different degrees of intelligence, patriotism, and virtue among the mass of the community, and their experience and proficiency in the art of self-government. Of these, the moral are, by far, the most influential. A community may possess all the necessary moral qualifications, in so high a degree, as to be capable of self-government under the most adverse circumstances; while, on the other hand, another may be so sunk in ignorance and vice, as to be incapable of forming a conception of liberty, or of living, even when most favored by circumstances, under any other than an absolute and despotic [government that has unlimited power] government.

Freedom Must Sometimes Be Limited

The principle, in all communities, according to these numerous and various causes, assigns to power and liberty their proper spheres. To allow to liberty, in any case, a sphere of action more extended than this assigns, would lead to anarchy; and this, probably, in the end, to a contraction instead of an enlargement of its sphere. Liberty, then, when forced on a people unfit for it, would, instead of a blessing, be a curse; as it would, in its reaction, lead directly to anarchy,—the greatest of all curses. No people, indeed, can long enjoy more liberty than that to which their situation and advanced intelligence and morals fairly entitle them. If more than this be allowed, they must soon fall into confusion and disorder,—to be followed, if not by anarchy [lack of all governance] and despotism, by a change to a form of government more simple and absolute; and, therefore, better suited to their condition. And hence, although it may be true, that a people may not have as much liberty as they are fairly entitled to, and are capable of enjoying,—yet the reverse is unquestionably true,—that no people can long possess more than they are fairly entitled to.

Liberty, indeed, though among the greatest of blessings, is not so great as that of protection; inasmuch, as the end of the former is the progress and improvement of the race,—

while that of the latter is its preservation and perpetuation [allowing something to continue]. And hence, when the two come into conflict, liberty must, and ever ought, to yield to protection; as the existence of the race is of greater moment than its improvement.

Freedom Is Dangerous When Given to the Undeserving

It follows, from what has been stated, that it is a great and dangerous error to suppose that all people are equally entitled to liberty. It is a reward to be earned, not a blessing to be gratuitously lavished on all alike;—a reward reserved for the intelligent, the patriotic, the virtuous and deserving;—and not a boon to be bestowed on a people too ignorant, degraded and vicious, to be capable either of appreciating or of enjoying it. Nor is it any disparagement [lessening] to liberty, that such is, and ought to be the case. On the contrary, its greatest praise,—its proudest distinction is, that an all-wise Providence has reserved it, as the noblest and highest reward for the development of our faculties, moral and intellectual. A reward more appropriate than liberty could not be conferred on the deserving;—nor a punishment inflicted on the undeserving more just, than to be subject to lawless and despotic rule. This dispensation seems to be the result of some fixed law;—and every effort to disturb or defeat it, by attempting to elevate a people in the scale of liberty, above the point to which they are entitled to rise, must ever prove abortive, and end in disappointment. The progress of a people rising from a lower to a higher point in the scale of liberty, is necessarily slow;—and by attempting to precipitate, we either retard, or permanently defeat it.

One Can Have Liberty Without Equality

There is another error, not less great and dangerous, usually associated with the one which has just been considered. I refer to the opinion, that liberty and equality are so intimately united, that liberty cannot be perfect without perfect equality.

That they are united to a certain extent,—and that equality of citizens, in the eyes of the law, is essential to liberty in a popular government, is conceded. But to go further, and make equality of *condition* essential to liberty, would be to destroy both liberty and progress. The reason is, that inequality of condition, while it is a necessary consequence of liberty, is, at the same time, indispensable to progress. In order to understand why this is so, it is necessary to bear in mind, that the main spring to progress is, the desire of individuals to better their condition; and that the strongest impulse which can be given to it is, to leave individuals free to exert themselves in the manner they may deem best for that purpose, as far at least as it can be done consistently with the ends for which government is ordained,—and to secure to all the fruits of their exertions. Now, as individuals differ greatly from each other, in intelligence, sagacity [wisdom], energy, perseverance, skill, habits of industry and economy, physical power, position and opportunity,—the necessary effect of leaving all free to exert themselves to better their condition, must be a corresponding inequality between those who may possess these qualities and advantages in a high degree, and those who may be deficient in them. The only means by which this result can be prevented are, either to impose such restrictions on the exertions of those who may possess them in a high degree, as will place them on a level with those who do not; or to deprive them of the fruits of their exertions. But to impose such restrictions on them would be destructive of liberty,—while, to deprive them of the fruits of their exertions, would be to destroy the desire of bettering their condition. It is, indeed, this inequality of condition between the front and rear ranks, in the march of progress, which gives so strong an impulse to the former to maintain their position, and to the latter to press forward into their files. This gives to progress its greatest impulse. To force the front rank back to the rear, or attempt to push forward the rear into line with the front, by the interposition [involvement] of the government, would put an end to the impulse, and effectually arrest the march of progress.

Believing All People Are Equal Is Wrong

These great and dangerous errors have their origin in the prevalent opinion that all men are born free and equal;—than which nothing can be more unfounded and false. It rests upon the assumption of a fact, which is contrary to universal observation, in whatever light it may be regarded. It is, indeed, difficult to explain how an opinion so destitute of all sound reason, ever could have been so extensively entertained, unless we regard it as being confounded with another, which has some semblance of truth;—but which, when properly understood, is not less false and dangerous. I refer to the assertion, that all men are equal in the state of nature; meaning, by a state of nature, a state of individuality, supposed to have existed prior to the social and political state; and in which men lived apart and independent of each other. If such a state ever did exist, all men would have been, indeed, free and equal in it; that is, free to do as they pleased, and exempt from the authority or control of others—as, by supposition, it existed anterior [before] to society and government. But such a state is purely hypothetical. It never did, nor can exist; as it is inconsistent with the preservation and perpetuation of the race. It is, therefore, a great misnomer [inaccurate name] to call it *the state of nature.* Instead of being the natural state of man, it is, of all conceivable states, the most opposed to his nature—most repugnant [offensive] to his feelings, and most incompatible with his wants. His natural state is, the social and political—the one for which his Creator made him, and the only one in which he can preserve and perfect his race. As, then, there never was such a state as the, so called, state of nature, and never can be, it follows, that men, instead of being born in it, are born in the social and political state; and of course, instead of being born free and equal, are born subject, not only to parental authority, but to the laws and institutions of the country where born, and under whose protection they draw their first breath.

4

A Debate on Whether the Declaration Includes Negroes

Abraham Lincoln and Stephen Douglas

Much of the argument in the October 7, 1858, debate in Galesburg, Illinois, between Abraham Lincoln and Stephen Douglas pivoted around whether the passage about the equality of all men in the Declaration of Independence included Negroes. Stephen Douglas was the incumbent senator of Illinois and Abraham Lincoln his challenger for the seat. Douglas maintained that Thomas Jefferson, a slaveholder himself, meant only white men of European descent when he said all men were created equal. On the contrary, Lincoln insisted, never once had Jefferson or any man since proven that blacks did not deserve equality, life, liberty, and the pursuit of happiness. Unlike Douglas, who believed that whether or not to hold slaves was a matter of personal choice, Lincoln maintained that slavery was morally wrong and must be abolished. At the time of these debates, Illinois, like many other states in the Union, was embroiled in a conflict over whether to remain a slaveholding state or to become a free state. Though Lincoln would lose the senatorial election of 1858, the publication of this and the six other senatorial debates between Douglas and him would help Lincoln win the presidential election of 1860.

Douglas: Now I ask you, my friends, why can't public men avow their principles alike everywhere? I would despise myself if I thought that I were seeking your votes by

Abraham Lincoln and Stephen Douglas, "The Fifth Joint Debate at Galesburg, October 7, 1858," *The Lincoln-Douglas Debates: The First Complete, Unexpurgated Text*, edited by Harold Holzer, New York: HarperCollins Publishers, 1993.

concealing my opinions, or advocating one set of principles in one part of the State and a different class in another part of the State. If I do not truly and honorably represent your feelings I ought not to be your Senator, and I will never conceal my opinions, or modify them, or change them and waste breath in order to get votes. I tell you that in my opinion this . . . doctrine of Mr. Lincoln's declaring that negroes and white men were included alike in the Declaration of Independence, made equal by Divine Providence, is a monstrous heresy. The signers of the Declaration of Independence never dreamed of the negro when they were writing that document. They referred to white men, men of European birth and European descent, when they declared the equality of all men. I see a gentleman here shaking his head. Let me remind him that when Thomas Jefferson wrote that Declaration he was the owner, and continued to [be to] the end of his life the owner of a large number of slaves. Did he intend to say that his negro slaves were created his equals by Divine law, and that he was violating the law of God every time of his life by holding them as slaves? Bear in mind that when that Declaration was put forth every one of the thirteen Colonies were slaveholding Colonies, and every man who signed the Declaration of Independence represented a slaveholding constituency. Bear in mind that no one of them emancipated [freed] his slaves, much less put them on an equality with himself when he signed the Declaration. On the contrary, they continued to hold them as slaves during the entire Revolutionary war. Now do you believe that? Are you willing to have it said that every man who signed the Declaration of Independence declared the negro his equal, and then was hypocrite enough to hold him as his slave in violation of what he believed to be Divine law? And yet when you say that the Declaration of Independence included the negro you charge the signers of the Declaration of Independence with hypocrisy. Now I say to you frankly that in my opinion this Government was made by our fathers on the white basis. It was made by white men for the benefit of white men and their posterity forever, and was intended to be administered in all time to come by white men. But while I hold that under our Constitution and political system the negro is not a citizen—cannot be a citizen—ought not to be a citizen—yet it don't follow by any means that he should be a slave. On the contrary, it does follow that the negro as an inferior race ought to possess every privilege, every immunity which he can safely exercise consistent with the good of society where he lives. Humanity requires, Christianity commands that you shall extend to every inferior being and every dependent race all the privileges, all the immunities and all the advantages which can be granted to him consistent with the safety of society. Again you ask me what is the nature and extent of these rights and privileges. My answer to that question is this: It is a question which the people of each State must decide for themselves. Illinois has decided that question for herself. We have said that in this State the negro shall not be a slave, nor shall he be a citizen. Kentucky holds a different doctrine, New York holds one different from either. Maine is different from all the rest, Virginia differs in many respects from each of the others, and so on. There are hardly two States whose policy is precisely alike in regard to the relation of the white man with the negro. You cannot reconcile them and make them alike. Each must do as it pleases. Illinois has as much right to adopt the policy we have on this subject as Kentucky has to a different policy. The great principle of this government is that each State has a right to do as it pleases on all these questions, and that no other power on earth has a right to interfere with us or complain of us merely because our system differs from theirs.

Slavery Issues Should Be Decided by Individual States

In the Compromise measures of 1850, Mr. [Henry] Clay recognized the great principle which I have asserted, and again in the Kansas–Nebraska Bill of 1854, that this same privilege ought to be extended into the Territories as well as the States. But Mr. Lincoln cannot be made to understand, and those who are determined to vote for him, no matter which side, whether in the North or South, whether for negro equality at one end of the State or against it at another—you cannot make one of them understand how it is that in a Territory the people can do as they please on the slavery question under the Dred Scott decision [in which a slave sought his freedom in the courts]. Let us see if I cannot make all impartial men see how that is. Chief Justice [Roger B.] Taney has said in his opinion in the Dred Scott case, that the negro slave being property, stands on an equal footing with other property and that the owner may carry them to a United States Territory the same as he does other property. Now suppose two of you, neighbors, concluded to go to Kansas. Suppose one should have a hundred negro slaves, and the other a hundred dollars' worth of mixed merchandise including a quantity of liquors, you both, according to that decision, may carry your property to Kansas. When you get there, the merchant with his liquors meets the Maine Liquor Law which forbids him to use or sell his property when he gets it there. What is this right to carry it there worth, if unfriendly legislation renders it useless and worthless when he gets there? How can the owner of the slave be more fortunate? The slaveholder, when he gets there, finds there is no local law, no slave code, no police regulation supporting and sustaining his right as a slaveholder, and he finds at once that the absence of friendly legislation excludes him just as positively and irresistibly as a positive constitutional prohibition could exclude him. Thus you find with any kind of property in a Territory, that it depends for its protection on the local and municipal law. Hence if the people of a Territory want slavery they will make friendly legislation to introduce it. If they don't want it, they will withhold all protection from it, and then it can't exist there. Such was the view of Southern men when the Nebraska bill passed. Read the speech of Mr. [James L.] Orr, of South Carolina, the present Speaker of Congress, and there you find this whole doctrine argued out at full length which I have now advanced. Read the speeches of other Senators and Representatives, and you will find they understood the Kansas-Nebraska bill in that way at that time, and hence slavery never could be force[d] on a people who didn't want it. I hold that in this country there is no power, there should be no power on the globe that can force any institution on an unwilling people. The great fundamental principle is that the people of each State and each Territory shall be left free to decide for themselves what shall be the nature and character of our institutions. This Government was based on that principle. When this Government was made there were twelve Slaveholding States and one Free State in this Union. Suppose this doctrine of Mr. Lincoln and the Republicans of uniformity on the subject of slavery in the laws of all the States had prevailed when this Government was made. Suppose Mr. Lincoln had been a member of the Convention that made the Constitution of the United States and that he had risen in that august body and addressing the father of his country, had said . . . "a house divided against itself cannot stand, this Government divided into Free and Slave States cannot permanently endure, that they must be all free or all slave, all the one thing or all the other," what do you think would have been the result? (I don't pretend to quote his exact language but I give his idea.) Suppose he had made that Convention believe that doctrine, and they had acted upon that, what would have been the result? Do you think that one Free State would have out-voted the twelve Slaveholding States and have abolished slavery therefrom[?] On the contrary, would not the twelve Slaveholding States have out-voted the one Free State and under his doctrine have fastened slavery under a Constitutional provision on every inch of the American Republic[?] Thus you see that the doctrine which he advocated now, if proclaimed at the beginning of the Government would have fashioned slavery everywhere throughout the American continent. Are you willing now since we have become the majority to exercise a power which we never would have submitted to when we were in the minority[?] If the Southern States had attempted to control our institutions, and made the States all slave when they had the power, I ask you would you have submitted to it? If you would not, are you willing now since we have become the majority under the great principle of self government which allows each State to do as it pleases, are you prepared now to force the doctrine on them?

The Only Peaceful Solution Is Compromise

My friends, I say to you there is but one path of peace in this Republic, and that is to administer this Government as our fathers made it, divided into free States and slave States, allowing each State to decide for itself whether it wants slavery or not. If Illinois [which wanted slavery to be abolished] will settle the question for herself, mind her own business and let her neighbors alone, we will be at peace with our neighbors. If Kentucky and every other Southern State will settle the question to suit themselves, and mind their own business and let others alone, there will be peace between the North and the South, and the whole Union. I am told my hour is up. . . .

Lincoln: My Fellow Citizens: A very large portion of the speech which Judge Douglas has addressed to you has previously been delivered and put in print. I did not mean that for a hit upon the Judge at all. If not interrupted, I was going on to say that such an answer as I was able to make to a very large portion of it, had already been once made and put in print, and there is an opportunity already afforded—an opportunity has already been afforded, to see our respective views upon a large portion of the speech which has not been addressed to you.

This . . . doctrine of Mr. Lincoln's declaring that negroes and white men were included alike in the Declaration of Independence, made equal by Divine Providence, is a monstrous heresy.

I make these remarks for the purpose of excusing myself for not passing over the entire ground that he has gone over. I however desire to take some of the points that he has attended to, and ask your attention to them. I shall follow back upon some notes that I have taken, instead of beginning at the head and following them down.

The Negro Was Included in the Declaration of Independence

He has alluded to the Declaration of Independence, and has insisted that negroes are not meant by the term "men" in that Declaration of Independence, and that it is a slander upon the framers of that instrument to suppose that they so meant. He asks you if it is possible to believe that Mr. Jefferson, who penned the Declaration of Independence would have supposed himself as applying the language of that instrument to the negro race, and yet have held a portion of that negro race in slavery, and not at once have freed them! I have only to remark upon this point, briefly, for I shall not detain you or myself upon it, that I believe the entire records of the world from the date of the Declaration of Independence up to within three years ago, may be searched in vain for one single declaration from one single man, that the negro was not included in the Declaration of Independence. I think I may defy Douglas to show that he ever said so, therefore, I think I may defy Douglas to show that any President ever said so—that any member of Congress ever said so—that any man ever said so until the necessities of the Democratic party had to invent that declaration. And I will remind Judge Douglas and this audience, that while Mr. Jefferson was the owner of slaves, as he undoubtedly was, he, speaking on this very subject, used the strong language that he trembled for his country, when he remembered that God was just. I will offer the highest premium in my power to Judge Douglas, if he will show that he, in all his life, has ever uttered a sentiment akin to that sentiment of Jefferson's. . . .

Blacks Are Physically Unequal but Not Morally

The Judge will have it, if we do not confess that there is a sort of inequality between the black and the white people, that lets us make slaves of the black, that we must make wives of them. Now, I have all the while made a wide distinction between this. He, perhaps, by taking two parts of the same speech might show as great a contrast as he does here. I have all the while maintained that inasmuch as there is a physical inequality between the white and black, that the blacks must remain inferior; but I have always maintained that in the right to life, liberty, and the pursuit of happiness, they were our equals, and this declaration I have constantly made with reference to the abstract moral question which I suppose to be the proper question to consider, when we are legislating about a new country which is not at ready to be beset with the actual presence of slavery. I have insisted that in legislating for a new country where slavery does not exist, there is no just rule other than that of pure morality and pure abstract right; and with reference to legislating with regard to these new countries, this abstract maxim, the right to life, liberty, and the pursuit of happiness, are the first rules to be considered and referred to.

Now, there is no misunderstanding this except by men that are interested in misunderstanding. I have to trust to a reading community to judge whether I advance just views, or whether I state views that are revolutionary or hypocritical. I believe myself guilty of no such thing as the latter; and of course I cannot claim that I am entirely free from error in the views and principles that I advance. . . .

The Judge tells us in proceeding that he is opposed to making an odious distinction between the free and slave

States. I am altogether unaware that the Republicans are in favor of making any odious distinction between the free and the slave States; but there still is a difference, as I think, between Judge Douglas and the Republicans in this vicinity of thought. For instance—Well, that is very beautiful—I suppose that the real difference between Judge Douglas and his friends, on the one side, and the Republicans on the other hand is, that the Judge is not in favor of making any difference between slavery and liberty, that he is in favor of eradicating, he is in favor of pressing out of view, and out of existence, all preference for free over slave institutions, and, consequently, every sentiment that he utters, discards the idea that he is against slavery, every sentiment that emanates from him discards the idea that there is any wrong in slavery. Every thought that he utters will be seen to exclude the thought that there is anything wrong in slavery. You will take his speeches and get the short pointed sentiments expressed by him, that he does not care if slavery is voted up, or voted down, and such like, you will see at once it is a perfectly logical idea if you admit that slavery is not wrong, but if it is wrong, Judge Douglas cannot say that he don't care for a wrong being voted up. Judge Douglas declares that if any community wants slavery they can have it. He can logically say that, if he admits that there is no wrong in it, but he cannot say that, if he admits that there is wrong in it! He insists, upon the score of equality, that the owner of slaves and the owner of horses should be allowed to take them alike to new territory and hold them there. That is perfectly logical if the species of property is perfectly alike, but if you admit that one of them is wrong, then you cannot admit any equality between right and wrong. I believe that slavery is wrong, and in a policy springing from that belief that looks to the prevention of the enlargement of that wrong, and that looks at some time to there being an end of that wrong. The other sentiment is, that it is no wrong, and the policy springing from it that there is no wrong in its becoming bigger, and that there never will be any end of it. There is the difference between Judge Douglas and his friends and the Republican party.

I confess myself as belonging to that class in the country that believes slavery to be a moral and political wrong. I feel, having regard to all constitutional guards thrown around it, that I do nevertheless desire a policy that shall prevent the enlargement of it. I do look to that point of time when it shall come to an end. . . .

To Allow Slavery Harms the Declaration of Independence

I have said once before, and I will repeat it now, that when Mr. Clay was once answering an objection to the Colonization Society, that it had a tendency to the ultimate emancipation of slavery, he said that those who would repress all tendency to liberty and ultimate emancipation must do more than put down the benevolent efforts of the Colonization Society; they must "go back to the hour of our own liberty and independence, and muzzle the cannon that thunders its annual joyous return; that they must blow out the moral lights around us; that they must pervert the human soul, and eradicate the human soul and love of liberty, and then, and not till then, they could perpetuate slavery in this country."

I do think, and must repeat, because I think it—I do think that Judge Douglas and whoever teaches that the negro has no humble share in the Declaration of Independence, is going back to the hour of our own liberty and independence, and so far as in him lies, is muzzling the cannon that thunders its annual joyous return; that he is blowing out the moral lights around us, and perverting the human soul and eradicating from the human soul the love of liberty, and in every possible way, preparing the public mind with his vast influence for making that institution of slavery perpetual and national.

Chapter 3

The Declaration Defends the Rights of All

1

All Men and Women Are Created Equal

Elizabeth Cady Stanton, Susan B. Anthony, and Matilda Joslyn Gage

Many advocates of the antislavery movement were silenced because they were women. American feminists gathered in Seneca Falls, New York, in 1848 to hold the world's first women's rights convention. Like their abolitionist contemporaries, these women believed the Declaration of Independence to be the most compelling American political document written about human freedom. In writing the following declaration, which resulted from the convention, feminist leaders Elizabeth Cady Stanton, Susan B. Anthony, and Matilda Joslyn Gage paraphrased the Declaration of Independence sentence for sentence, first stating how the rights of women had been violated and second, how these rights should be defended. The document still stands today as one of the vanguards of the women's movement.

When, in the course of human events, it becomes necessary for one portion of the family of man to assume among the people of the earth a position different from that which they have hitherto occupied, but one to which the laws of nature and of nature's God entitle them, a decent respect to the opinions of mankind requires that they should declare the causes that impel them to such a course.

We hold these truths to be self-evident: that all men and women are created equal; that they are endowed by their Creator with certain inalienable rights; that among these

Elizabeth Cady Stanton, Susan B. Anthony, and Matilda Joslyn Gage, *History of Woman Suffrage*, New York: published by Elizabeth Cady Stanton, Susan B. Anthony, and Matilda Joslyn Gage, 1881.

are life, liberty, and the pursuit of happiness; that to secure these rights governments are instituted, deriving their just powers from the consent of the governed. Whenever any form of government becomes destructive of these ends, it is the right of those who suffer from it to refuse allegiance to it, and to insist upon the institution of a new government, laying its foundation on such principles, and organizing its powers in such form, as to them shall seem most likely to effect their safety and happiness. Prudence, indeed, will dictate that governments long established should not be changed for light and transient causes; and accordingly all experience hath shown that mankind are more disposed to suffer, while evils are sufferable, than to right themselves by abolishing the forms to which they were accustomed. But when a long train of abuses and usurpations, pursuing invariably the same object evinces a design to reduce them under absolute despotism, it is their duty to throw off such government, and to provide new guards for their future security. Such has been the patient sufferance of the women under this government, and such is now the necessity which constrains them to demand the equal station to which they are entitled.

Abuses Women Have Suffered

The history of mankind is a history of repeated injuries and usurpations on the part of man toward woman, having in direct object the establishment of an absolute tyranny over her. To prove this, let facts be submitted to a candid world.

But when a long train of abuses and usurpations, pursuing invariably the same object evinces a design to reduce them under absolute despotism, it is their duty to throw off such government, and to provide new guards for their future security.

He has never permitted her to exercise her inalienable right to the elective franchise [the vote].

He has compelled her to submit to laws, in the formation of which she had no voice.

He has withheld from her rights which are given to the

most ignorant and degraded men—both natives and foreigners.

Having deprived her of this first right of a citizen, the elective franchise, thereby leaving her without representation in the halls of legislation, he has oppressed her on all sides.

He has endeavored, in every way that he could, to destroy her confidence in her own powers, to lessen her self-respect, and to make her willing to lead a dependent and abject life.

He has made her, if married, in the eye of the law, civilly dead.

He has taken from her all right in property, even to the wages she earns.

He has made her, morally, an irresponsible being, as she can commit many crimes with impunity [without punishment], provided they be done in the presence of her husband. In the covenant of marriage, she is compelled to promise obedience to her husband, he becoming, to all intents and purposes, her master—the law giving him power to deprive her of her liberty, and to administer chastisement.

Women's Powers Are Limited

He has so framed the laws of divorce, as to what shall be the proper causes, and in case of separation, to whom the guardianship of the children shall be given, as to be wholly regardless of the happiness of women—the law, in all cases, going upon a false supposition of the supremacy of man, and giving all power into his hands.

After depriving her of all rights as a married woman, if single, and the owner of property, he has taxed her to support a government which recognizes her only when her property can be made profitable to it.

He has monopolized nearly all the profitable employments, and from those she is permitted to follow, she receives but a scanty remuneration. He closes against her all the avenues to wealth and distinction which he considers most honorable to himself. As a teacher of theology, medicine, or law, she is not known.

He has denied her the facilities for obtaining a thorough education, all colleges being closed against her.

He allows her in Church, as well as State, but a subordinate position, claiming Apostolic [Biblical or Church] authority for her exclusion from the ministry, and, with some exceptions, from any public participation in the affairs of the Church.

Women Are Made to Feel Bad About Themselves

He has created a false public sentiment by giving to the world a different code of morals for men and women, by which moral delinquencies which exclude women from society, are not only tolerated, but deemed of little account in man.

He has usurped [overthrown] the prerogative [special right or privilege] of Jehovah himself, claiming it as his right to assign for her a sphere of action, when that belongs to her conscience and to her God.

He has endeavored, in every way that he could, to destroy her confidence in her own powers, to lessen her self-respect, and to make her willing to lead a dependent and abject life.

Now, in view of this entire disfranchisement [depriving of legal rights] of one-half the people of this country, their social and religious degradation—in view of the unjust laws above mentioned, and because women do feel themselves aggrieved, oppressed, and fraudulently [illegally] deprived of their most sacred rights, we insist that they have immediate admission to all the rights and privileges which belong to them as citizens of the United States.

In entering upon the great work before us, we anticipate no small amount of misconception, misrepresentation, and ridicule; but we shall use every instrumentality within our power to effect our object. We shall employ agents, circulate tracts [pamphlets], petition the State and National legislatures, and endeavor to enlist the pulpit and the press in our behalf. We hope this Convention will be followed by a series of Conventions embracing every part of the country.

Resolutions to Correct Injustices

Whereas, The great precept of nature is conceded to be, that "man shall pursue his own true and substantial happiness."

Blackstone in his Commentaries remarks, that this law of Nature being coeval with mankind, and dictated by God himself, is of course superior in obligation to any other. It is binding over all the globe, in all countries and at all times; no human laws are of any validity if contrary to this, and such of them as are valid, derive all their force, and all their validity, and all their authority, mediately [indirectly related to] and immediately, from this original; therefore,

Resolved, That such laws as conflict, in any way, with the true and substantial happiness of woman, are contrary to the great precept of nature and of no validity, for this is "superior in obligation to any other."

Resolved, That all laws which prevent woman from occupying such a station in society as her conscience shall dictate, or which place her in a position inferior to that of man, are contrary to the great precept of nature, and therefore of no force or authority.

Resolved, That woman is man's equal—was intended to be so by the Creator, and the highest good of the race demands that she should be recognized as such.

Resolved, *That it is the duty of the women of this country to secure to themselves their sacred right to the elective franchise.*

Resolved, That the women of this country ought to be enlightened in regard to the laws under which they live, that they may no longer publish their degradation by declaring themselves satisfied with their present position, nor their ignorance, by asserting that they have all the rights they want.

Resolved, That inasmuch as man, while claiming for himself intellectual superiority, does accord to woman moral superiority, it is pre-eminently his duty to encourage her to speak and teach, as she has an opportunity, in all religious assemblies.

Resolved, That the same amount of virtue, delicacy, and refinement of behavior that is required of woman in the social state, should also be required of man, and the same transgressions [incorrect behavior] should be visited with equal severity on both man and woman.

Resolved, That the objection of indelicacy and impropriety, which is so often brought against woman when she addresses a public audience, comes with a very ill-grace from those who encourage, by their attendance, her appearance on the stage, in the concert, or in feats of the circus.

Resolved, That woman has too long rested satisfied in the circumscribed [controlled] limits which corrupt customs and a perverted application of the Scriptures have marked out for her, and that it is time she should move in the enlarged sphere which her great Creator has assigned her.

Resolved, That it is the duty of the women of this country to secure to themselves their sacred right to the elective franchise.

Resolved, That the equality of human rights results necessarily from the fact of the identity of the race in capabilities and responsibilities.

Resolved, therefore, That, being invested by the Creator with the same capabilities, and the same consciousness of responsibility for their exercise, it is demonstrably the right and duty of woman, equally with man, to promote every righteous cause by every righteous means; and especially in regard to the great subjects of morals and religion, it is self-evidently her right to participate with her brother in teaching them, both in private and in public, by writing and by speaking, by any instrumentalities proper to be used, and in any assemblies proper to be held; and this being a self-evident truth growing out of the divinely implanted principles of human nature, any custom or authority adverse to it, whether modern or wearing the hoary [gray, old] sanction of antiquity, is to be regarded as a self-evident falsehood, and at war with mankind.

The Declaration Defends the Rights of the Unborn

Mackubin Thomas Owens

Writer and college professor Mackubin Thomas Owens finds distinct similarities between the arguments pro-slavery advocates used to perpetuate the practice and those of the pro-abortionists today. In the following article, he describes how arguments that blacks were not human and therefore need not be freed have been used similarly to defend a woman's right to abort her fetus on the grounds that it is not a human and thus need not be considered in her decision. Owens, writing in 1996, urges that as Lincoln defended the rights of blacks by insisting that they were indeed human beings and protected under the free and equal passage in the Declaration of Independence, political leaders today should use the document to protect the rights of the unborn who are not only unquestionably human but equal in value to the women who conceived them.

Historical analogy is oftentimes a dangerous way of casting light on contemporary issues. After all, no two occurrences are ever exactly the same. But every now and then a parallel appears to be so compelling that it simply cannot be ignored. Similarities between the pro-slavery arguments made during the period leading up to the Civil War and those advanced today on behalf of abortion are surely a case in point.

One thing that history does show is that republics cannot function without a moral consensus on important issues. For Americans, the most important issue was and is the question

Mackubin Thomas Owens, "Let Us Re-Adopt the Declaration," *The Human Life Review*, Fall 1996.

of who is human, and thus who possesses the natural and equal rights to "life, liberty and the pursuit of happiness," as expressed in the Declaration of Independence, and which the Constitution was framed to protect. During the 1840s and 1850s, the focus of this question was the status of the black race in America. Today, it is the status of the unborn.

Lincoln, Calhoun Disagree over Natural Rights

During the decades leading up to the Civil War, defenders of slavery like John C. Calhoun [American politician and vice president from 1825–1832] essentially argued that the institution was justified because the natural rights laid out in the Declaration did not apply to the black race. In 1857, this position was given judicial sanction by Chief Justice Roger Taney in *Dred Scott v. Sandford.*

Taney declared that the founders could not have meant for the Declaration of Independence to include blacks and that, accordingly, whether enslaved or free, the black race had no rights that the white man was bound to respect; that slavery was a constitutionally protected right; and that . . . Congress could not prohibit the expansion of slavery into the federal territories.

Lincoln especially feared that—as a result of such a transformation in public sentiment away from support of the Declaration's principles of equality—free government could not survive.

Abraham Lincoln disagreed. He argued that the founders understood the Declaration of Independence to apply to all, that they compromised on the issue of slavery out of necessity, not because they believed it was right, and that the doctrines of Taney and Calhoun represented a repudiation of the "central idea" of the Declaration and thereby republican government. To Lincoln, slavery was an affront to republican government itself, leading "good men . . . into open war with the fundamental principles of civil liberty—criticizing the Declaration of Independence, and insisting that there is no right principle of action but self interest."

He feared that [political opponent Senator] Stephen

Douglas's doctrine of "popular sovereignty," which professed indifference to the moral aspects of slavery, and Taney's judicial institutionalization of Calhoun's racial doctrine were preparing public sentiment to accept the transformation of the slavery question from one of "hostility to the principle, and toleration, only by necessity" to slavery as a "sacred right." Lincoln especially feared that—as a result of such a transformation in public sentiment away from support of the Declaration's principles of equality—free government could not survive.

Slavery Debate Not Unlike One over Abortion

Roe v. Wade [the court case that resulted in legalized abortion] is the contemporary version of *Dred Scott.* In this case, the Supreme Court ruled that the unborn child has no rights that are bound to be respected by the already born. As the slave was the absolute property of the slaveholder, so the unborn child is merely "fetal matter" under the absolute control of a woman, and subject to "no right principle of action but self interest." As *Dred Scott* helped to shape public sentiment on behalf of the idea that slavery was a "sacred right" with which Congress could not interfere, *Roe v. Wade* has helped to shape public opinion in support of the belief that abortion is a woman's absolute right. This view is reinforced by the John Calhoun of the abortion movement, Kate Michelman, and the "ultras" [extremists] of the National Abortion and Reproductive Rights League.

Like slavery, the debate over abortion is frequently couched in terms of "choice." Sen. Douglas was "pro-choice" on slavery. For instance, he argued that the issue of slavery in Kansas was no different from the issue of selling liquor in Maine. But abortion, like slavery, is a moral issue. While disagreements among reasonable people about liquor laws—or taxes, welfare spending and the like—can lead to compromise, there can be no such "middle ground" on moral issues. Slavery and abortion are either evil or they are not. In Lincoln's words, to seek a "middle ground between the right and the wrong [is as] vain as the search for a man who should be neither a living man or a dead man."

As Lincoln recognized, moral indifference to such issues as slavery and abortion cannot help but have an adverse influence on self-government itself. As he said of Douglas during their first joint debate:

> When he invites any people, willing to have slavery, to establish it, he is blowing out the moral lights around us. When he says he "cares not whether slavery is voted up or voted down"—that it is a sacred right of self-government—he is, in my judgement, penetrating the human soul and eradicating the light of reason and the love of liberty in this American people.

Perhaps these words ought to be contemplated by such "pro-choice" Republicans as Massachusetts Governor William Weld, New Jersey Governor Christine Todd Whitman, and California Governor Pete Wilson, who are playing the role of Douglas in today's debate over abortion.

Clinging to a rhetoric about abortion in which there is no life and no death, we entangle our beliefs in a series of self-delusions, fibs and evasions.

The similarities between slavery and abortion do not end here. They extend to the related political and social issues as well. Advocates of slavery argued that the institution was a "positive good" and that, indeed, slaves were better off than the free laborers of the North. Just so, advocates of abortion contend that abortion is preferable to life in poverty, or as an "unwanted child." Echoing the very language of Calhoun regarding slavery, Beverly Harrison, a professor of Christian Ethics at Union Theological Seminary, contends that abortion is a "positive good" and can even be a "loving choice" for a woman.

Opposition Voices Silenced

In the 1840s and 1850s, the Democratic Party was held hostage by the "slave power." Today, it is the "abortion power" that dominates the agenda of the Democrats so completely that the pro-life Democratic former Governor of Pennsylvania, Robert Casey, was not even allowed to address the 1992 Democratic Party convention (he was refused a hearing again this year [1996] as well).

In the 1850s, the Democrats put Republicans on the defensive by associating them with the violence of abolitionists like John Brown. Today, in a similar attempt to silence and coerce those who disagree with the pro-abortion stance, Democrats equate opposition to abortion with the violence of extremists like John Salvi, who have killed workers in abortion clinics.

But the slave power overreached. This overreaching began as early as 1857, when pro-choice Democrats like Douglas were enraged by the slavepower's attempt, in concert with President James Buchanan, to coerce the nation into accepting the admission of Kansas as a slave state on the basis of the fraudulent pro-slavery Lecompton Constitution. It continued with the demand for a sedition law that would, in Lincoln's words, suppress "all declarations that slavery is wrong, whether made in politics, in presses, in pulpits, or in private . . ."

Today, the abortion power seems to be on the verge of a similar overreaching. A case in point is the current "sedition law" that essentially outlaws anti-abortion protests. Another is the recent veto by President Clinton of a congressional attempt to ban "partial birth" abortions. In the words of the Democrat Senator from New York, Daniel Patrick Moynihan, who voted to override the president's veto, partial birth abortions are "just too close to infanticide." Another is the British case in which a healthy twin fetus was aborted simply because the mother wanted only one more child.

The Right to Kill

Yet another is the hardening of the abortion power's official position that the fetus is not really an unborn child, and that there is no moral component to ending a fetal life other than the absolute right of the mother "to choose" killing it.

This last position was harshly criticized by the pro-choice feminist writer (and new mother) Naomi Wolf in a 1995 issue of the *New Republic.* She argued that the pro-choice movement has lost its "ethical core" and indeed something more. In words eerily reminiscent of Lincoln's during the first debate with Douglas, cited above, she wrote that

> we [of the pro-choice movement] stand in jeopardy of losing what can only be called our souls. Clinging to a rhetoric about abortion in which there is no life and no death, we entangle our beliefs in a series of self-delusions, fibs and evasions. And we risk becoming precisely what our critics charge us with being: callous,

selfish and casually destructive men and women who share a cheapened view of life.

What does the slavery-abortion analogy imply for the future policy of the pro-life movement? Again, Lincoln provides a guide: the education of public opinion. "In this and like communities," Lincoln said during his first debate, "public sentiment is everything." With public sentiment, nothing can fail; without it nothing can succeed. Consequently he who molds public sentiment, goes deeper than he who enacts statutes or pronounces decisions. He makes statutes or decisions possible or impossible to be executed.

Equality Should Apply to the Unborn

Nearly two years earlier, Lincoln had observed that public opinion on any subject, always has a "central idea," from which all its minor thoughts radiate. That "central idea" in our political public opinion, at the beginning was, and until recently has continued to be, "the equality of men." And although it was always submitted patiently to whatever of inequality there seemed to be as a matter of practical necessity, its constant working has been a steady progress toward the practical equality of all men.

The goal of the pro-life movement should be to shape opinion on behalf of the understanding that equality, the "central idea" of America, applies to the unborn.

Almost 24 years after *Roe*, this educational process has finally begun. Although the Senate failed to overturn President Clinton's veto of the ban on partial-birth abortions, the campaign against this procedure has served to shift the terms of the debate from "a woman's right to an abortion" to the rights of the unborn child. The abortion power understands the crucial—indeed, potentially decisive—importance of this shift. In the words of Kate Michelman, "there is no question that the anti-choice movement's strategy was to reposition the debate, to get the focus away from women and women's choices and their moral right to make a choice, to the fetus. I do not think it is successful among the general public."

But Ms. Michelman is whistling past the cemetery. The majority of Americans have been able and willing to avoid treating abortion as a moral issue because the abortion power has been successful in claiming that the fetus is not a baby—which, ironically, ignores the fact that "fetus" is the

Latin word for child or "offspring"! But the partial-birth abortion debate has now made it difficult, if not impossible, for the abortion power to maintain this fiction.

It is of course true that the anti-abortion position has long had substantial support: in 1994, for instance, not one pro-life incumbent [a candidate who currently holds a position and is seeking reelection to it] lost to a pro-abortion challenger in the congressional elections. In my judgment, if the pro-life movement follows a measured approach, focusing on the humanity of the fetus while eschewing [rejecting] all-or-nothing strategies such as the attempt to outlaw abortion by amending the Constitution, it will be able to drive a wedge between the horror of abortion and the decent citizens of the United States. The outcome will be the continued growth of moral consensus in support of the anti-abortion position.

Abortion Corrupts the Political System

It will grow as more citizens come to realize that abortion, like slavery, is an affront to republican government, that it violates the "central idea" of America: commitment to the equal natural rights expressed in the Declaration of Independence. It is especially this connection between abortion and republican government that anti-abortionists must drive home: How can the decent citizens of a decent regime tolerate abortion? How can they be indifferent to the millions of unborn lives terminated over the past two decades, often if not usually for no reason but self-interest and convenience?

Lincoln's words at Peoria in his speech on the Kansas-Nebraska Act apply as much to abortion today as they did to slavery in 1854.

> Our republican robe is soiled, and trailed in the dust. Let us turn and wash it white in the spirit, if not the blood, of the Revolution. . . . Let us re-adopt the Declaration of Independence, and with it, the practices, and policy, which harmonize it. . . . If we do this, we shall not only have saved the Union; but we shall have so saved it, as to make, and to keep it, forever worthy of the saving. We shall have so saved it, that the succeeding millions of free happy people, the world over, shall rise up, and call us blessed, to the last generation.

The failure to do so will mean that the "moral lights" will continue to go out, and that republican government will become little more than a husk.

The Declaration Obligates the Government to Protect Americans' Rights

James Garbarino

Throughout the history of the United States, people have sharply disagreed over whether the family should be considered a private or a public entity. Their answers have determined whether or not they believe government should intervene to secure the welfare of children and their parents. James Garbarino, director of Cornell University's Family Life Development Center, said in the following article that many children and mothers and the structure of the family itself have suffered from the same social ills for more than one hundred years. He maintains that though the government should not excessively interfere with families, it must ensure the basic human rights of each family and each person within a family. In fact, Garbarino asserts that the Declaration of Independence, as one of the pivotal documents in U.S. history, dictates that the defense of each citizen is to be of the utmost importance. Though he argues primarily from the arena of family policy, he insists that the primary goal of the government should be to extend basic human rights to those who have had them denied in the past—women, children, the non-white, and homosexuals.

There is much to learn from the parallels that exist between the concerns of family policy today and family policy one full century ago.

James Garbarino, "A Vision of Family Policy for the 21st Century," *Journal of Social Studies*, Fall 1996, pp. 197–204.

This is not the first time I have been down this path. A few years ago I was asked to deliver an address on the occasion of the 100th anniversary of the founding of a family service association in Chicago. To prepare myself for that assignment I sat in a public park in the city that had been in operation for 100 years, and I consulted a sample of newspapers from that era. The exercise was illuminating.

Family Policy Issues of the 1890s

The issues relevant to family policy that are before me as I imagined myself transported back to 1893 were these, among others:

1. The problem of substance abuse and addiction was recognized as an insidious and powerful destructive force in family life.
2. There was evidence of a widening gap between rich and poor, and already many voices called for action to improve the conditions of the poor, particularly the "worthy" poor.
3. Traditional American values and institutions were being challenged by the influx of immigrants who did not speak English and who were perceived to make disproportionate demands on the human service systems, suppressing wages by accepting low pay, long hours, and inferior working conditions.
4. The legacy of slavery and the reality of racism lurked behind the public facade of democracy, and broke out in dramatic incidents that captured front page headlines from time to time.
5. Growing numbers of girls and women were judged to be in moral jeopardy due to the frequency of premarital sex and pregnancy, and the sex industry in fact flourished.
6. Child abuse was entering the public consciousness and there was a sense that juvenile crime was escalating.
7. Significant numbers of families were not intact, as mothers frequently died in childbirth and fathers often abandoned families.

Family Policy Issues of the Present

Does this sound familiar? . . .

The more things change, the more they remain the

same? Does anything ever really change? Or is it just the characters and not the plot?. . . There have been changes in the past 100 years: divorce and unmarried teen births have replaced maternal death and paternal separation in the dynamic of "incomplete" families; overtly homosexual adults now assert claims on parental roles without apology; efforts to integrate employment and maternity have become commonplace concerns of employers large and small; and a structural analysis that construes child abuse as a social—rather than a personal—problem has taken hold among the experts. These are real changes, of course, and they demand policy adjustments and innovations at all levels of public life.

The legacy of slavery and the reality of racism lurked behind the public facade of democracy, and broke out in dramatic incidents that captured front page headlines from time to time.

Yet in our efforts to understand the current policy agenda, let us not forget that some of the essential elements of that agenda have deep roots in the American experience. After all, it was as we approached the 20th century that some of the major themes. . . first were laid down. These themes include attention to the costs and benefits of industrialization and of a global economy, multiculturalism [integration of numerous ethnic backgrounds]; calls for and criticism of "big government," a human rights perspective on racism, the costs of militarism and empire expansion; the emergence and impact of "mass" media, and the quest for the prototypic [typical] American family.

In 1896, the United States was being transformed by the seemingly unstoppable social logic of industrialism, and the country fast was becoming a major player in the global economy. . . . New economic relationships emerged between husbands and wives, and young girls became independent economic entities as they entered the cash economy. Throughout this transformation, the look of America changed dramatically as we embarked on the process of moving activities from the "non-monetarized" [not driven by money] to the "monetarized" economies and from our agrarian past to an urban social model of family and society.

Public vs. Private Interests

It was then, 100 years ago, that progressive elements in American society began to assert "big government" was required as a counterforce to "big business," if America's commitment to human rights was to be preserved. As private industrial and financial entities grew in size and scope, they began to absorb and to radiate a political power that was outside the scope envisioned by the nation's founding fathers. This development provided the foundation for a constitutional crisis that pitted an ideology of small government and a narrow interpretation of the Constitution against an interpretation that stressed the elasticity of the Constitution and the need to grow government to preserve the rights of life, liberty, and the pursuit of happiness amid the complexities of a modern industrial society.

The social contract model implies mutual obligations and rights, and so it provides a strong moral imperative for public efforts to ensure the safety and quality of the child's experience.

The 1890s saw the initial creation of Imperial America—the America of the military-industrial complex that projected power globally and that imposed a market focus upon foreign policy. At the same time, America was challenged to refine the meaning of its core identity as an Anglo culture. Defacto bilingualism [though not officially recognized many people spoke both English and their native language] in schools and neighborhoods contested with a strong "nativist" streak—an ironic term given the fact that truly Native-Americans were completely excluded from this culture. All this was taking place in the context of "the closing of the American frontier" as Frederick Jackson Turner conclusively defined it in 1893. Gradually this "closing" symbolically, and increasingly literally, shut off the spigot that previously released the disaffected [discontented with authority] citizenry into the open lands of the west, where there was freedom to exert individualism rather than the necessity to address and resolve social conflict. The result, which has been increasing confrontation about social issues, has become engrained in our social discourse today.

Finally, the rise of a mass media emerged as a mechanism for creating a truly national conciousness . . . through the generation and mass dissemination [distribution] of images shared by all who read, listen to, and watch the same material. Current analyses of television, movies, and other homogenizing cultural forces find their parallels a century ago, when American families first became part of a national experience of fashion, issue definition, and event sharing. This transformation, from individualist to shared input and experience, offered the models for today's national culture in which mass communication conveys information in real time, and in which television families have become realer than real.

There is much more that could be said about the late 19th century and its relevance to understanding our approach to the 21st, but this sketch must suffice. Turning to the core issues that characterize current and future efforts to wrestle with family policy, the central or organizing theme of contemporary debate is the ongoing struggle between individualist and collectivist [political ideas that advocate group control over people and the economy] conceptualizations of the family's role and responsibilities.

Opposing Visions of the Family's Role in Community

At the heart of this debate is the matter of how and when families are private and how and when they are public. This question lurks behind conceptualizations of child maltreatment as "the price of privacy," as well as behind many decisions of law and policy in which children are presumed to be citizens with a primary relationship to the state, or private members of families with no direct link to the state under ordinary circumstances, or private property of their adult parents. Some societies define families as child-rearing agents of the state, as did the former USSR. Others see families as the primary unit of society, and the state as having authority over children or any other facet of family function in cases of "last resort."

This latter vision characterizes biological conception as tantamount [equal] to entering into a contract with the community: the social contract model implies mutual obligations and rights, and so it provides a strong moral imperative for public efforts to ensure the safety and quality of the child's experience. The opposing vision validates a voluntary . . . model of the relationship between families and the state. These opposing visions are represented in contemporary policy debate about issues like child welfare (is it an entitlement? a privilege? a tool for social control?), teen pregnancy (who has authority over a girl who gets pregnant? over the child?), divorce and child support (is financial responsibility for a child purely a private contract between divorced adults, or a public responsibility?), and other issues. . . .

Here is the fundamental contract with America, the truly revolutionary principle that governments exist to secure basic human rights.

The question of how and when families are publicly versus privately obligated or empowered, and that of the relationship between families and the government and community, cluster around the meaning of a social support system. [American sociologist] Gerald Caplan developed the concept of a social support system in the context of community mental health as a network of entities, processes, and expectations that combine feedback and nurturance—that is, social support systems evaluate an individual's behavior on behalf of society and offer psychological resources to the individual as a matter of that person's human rights. A social support system is not simply the unconditional provision of resources. Rather, it is the provision of resources in the context of monitoring, standard setting, and other dimensions of social control. In this rendition a social support system is not the financial safety net nor the formal social services of government qua [as in] Big Brother [attempt to control people completely through government], but perhaps as "Big Sister," not authoritarian but caring. Perhaps this is one reason why the most effective family support program is the home health visitor program. Home health visitors exemplify the Big Sister features of being a social support system: they offer resources and they represent the interests and the standards of the community vis-a-vis [through] the family.

The Government's Role in Family Life

But is social support a public obligation? This is the essential question that pervades much of current policy debate, much as it did 100 years ago and probably will in the coming decades. On one side of this debate are those who argue that families are essentially private and that the role of government in their care and feeding must be minimal, limited to the very most basic matters of child protection. This is certainly the moving spirit behind the "Contract with America" offered by the Republicans in the 1994 elections, which echoed the [George] Bush administration's concept of "1000 points of light" [the phrase used to encourage people to volunteer their time and talents] and other formulations that focus on the privatization of human services and economic affairs. Is this the American foundation for family policy? Does the government stand outside the family as a bystander, perhaps intervening . . . when there is no other last resort in the "private sector?" Is there an authentically American answer to this question? I think there is, and that it lies with the original contract with America.

What is the original contract with America, the touchstone for American public policy debate? It is the Declaration of Independence, for in this document is found the essential premise of American ideology. That premise is the assertion that "We hold these truths to be self-evident, that all men are created equal, that they are endowed by their creator with certain unalienable rights, that among these are life, liberty, and the pursuit of happiness." This assertion of human rights was itself dramatically innovative for its time.

Government Exists to Ensure Equality

The most important ideological innovation of the Declaration, however, was contained not in this statement of rights, but rather in the words that followed, which identified the reason for government. Specifically, the Declaration states "[t]hat to secure these rights governments are instituted. . . ." Here is the fundamental contract with America, the truly revolutionary principle that governments exist to secure basic human rights. The best of American history has been the refinement and the application of this contract, including efforts to rectify the original omissions of the rights of females and of people of color. This revolutionary conception of government, as the guarantor of human rights, is the starting point for our discussions of family policy. From here we must be clear that government exists not to protect the rich or any other elite, nor to make the world safe for big business, nor to facilitate greed or self-interest, nor to promote a religious group's narrow agenda. Rather, the founders of the nation stated that the basic purpose of government is to secure basic human rights, unalienable rights. This is the appeal for those who would insist that public policy support the parental aspirations of homosexuals, that dangerous neighborhoods be restored to safety so children can escape trauma and abuse, and that the needs of children remain paramount [of extreme importance] even as economic structures change. . . .

When the current empirical [visible] evidence is placed within the revolutionary spirit of the original contract with America, the conclusion seems clear. The best of American history lies in successful efforts to broaden the reach of human rights to the female and the non-White, and so it will be that the best of our future will be found in efforts to align the resources of government in ways that ensure new family forms, and that ensure families in new social contexts can function at their best on behalf of life, liberty, and the pursuit of happiness. Whether it be stepfamilies, gay-lesbian families, dual-career families, teen families, or families living in high stress neighborhood environments, children can thrive if they and their parents live in settings that reflect a policy of respect, validation, and support.

Blacks Shall Declare Their Own Independence

National Committee of Black Churchmen

In 1970, after more than 350 years in America, blacks still were not treated as the equals of whites. Not even the Civil Rights movement of the 1960s had secured significant changes in their status. Originally published in the July 3, 1970, edition of *The New York Times* and written by a group of black clergy called the National Committee of Black Churchmen, the following Black Declaration of Independence specifies a list of abuses blacks have suffered in the past and at the time of its writing. It also points out the numerous peaceful and unsuccessful appeals for blacks made to the U.S. government. Though its authors do not encourage violence as a means of gaining rights for blacks, they do make a revolutionary call for blacks to disrupt the systems in government that perpetuate their mistreatment. They maintain that blacks should neither keep silent about the abuses they suffer nor remain loyal and obedient to a nation that does not extend to them the same rights it does other citizens.

In the Black Community, July 4, 1970 A Declaration by Concerned Black Citizens of the United States of America in Black Churches, Schools, Homes, Community Organizations and Institutions assembled:

When in the course of Human Events, it becomes necessary for a People who were stolen from the lands of their

National Committee of Black Churchmen, "Black Declaration of Independence," *The New York Times*, July 3, 1970.

Fathers, transported under the most ruthless and brutal circumstances 5,000 miles to a strange land, sold into dehumanizing slavery, emasculated, subjugated, exploited and discriminated against for 351 years, to call, with finality, a halt to such indignities and genocidal practices—by virtue of the Laws of Nature and of Nature's God, a decent respect to the Opinions of Mankind requires that they should declare their just grievances and the urgent and necessary redress thereof.

We hold these truths to be self-evident, that all Men are not *only* created equal and endowed by their Creator with certain unalienable rights among which are Life, Liberty and the Pursuit of Happiness, but that when this equality and these rights are deliberately and consistently refused, withheld or abnegated [denied], men are bound by self-respect and honor to rise up in righteous indignation to secure them. Whenever any Form of Government, or any variety of established traditions and systems of the Majority becomes destructive of Freedom and of legitimate Human Rights, it is the Right of the Minorities to use every necessary and accessible means to protest and to disrupt the machinery of Oppression, and so to bring such general distress and discomfort upon the oppressor as to the offended Minorities shall seem most appropriate and most likely to effect a proper adjustment of the society.

Blacks Have Been Patient Too Long

Prudence, indeed, will dictate that such bold tactics should not be initiated for light and transient Causes; and, accordingly, the Experience of White America has been that the descendants of the African citizens brought forcibly to these shores, and to the shores of the Caribbean Islands, as slaves have been patient long past what can be expected of any human beings so affronted. But when a long train of Abuses and Violence, pursuing invariably the same Object, manifests a Design to reduce them under Absolute Racist Domination and Injustice, it is their Duty radically to confront such Government or system of traditions, and to provide, under the aegis [control or guidance] of Legitimate Minority Power and Self Determination, for their present Relief and future Security. Such has been the patient Sufferance of Black People in the United States of America; and such is now the Necessity which constrains them to address this

Declaration to Despotic White Power, and to give due notice of their determined refusal to be any longer silenced by fear or flattery, or to be denied justice. The history of the treatment of Black People in the United States is a history having in direct Object the Establishment and Maintenance of Racist Tyranny over this People. To prove this, let Facts be submitted to a candid World.

List of Grievances

The United States has evaded Compliance to laws the most wholesome and necessary for our Children's education.

The United States has caused us to be isolated in the most dilapidated and unhealthful sections of all cities.

The United States has allowed election districts to be so gerrymandered [divided to benefit those who did the dividing] the Black People find the right to Representation in the Legislatures almost impossible of attainment.

The United States has allowed the dissolution [destruction by breaking down] of school districts controlled by Blacks when Blacks opposed with manly Firmness the white man's Invasions on the Rights of our People.

The United States has erected a Multitude of Public Agencies and Offices, and sent into our ghettos Swarms of Social Workers, Officers and Investigators to harass our People, and eat out their substance to feed the Bureaucracies.

The United States has kept in our ghettoes, in Times of Peace, Standing Armies of Police, State Troopers and National Guardsmen, without the consent of our People.

The United States has imposed Taxes upon us without protecting our Constitutional Rights.

It is the Right of the Minorities to use every necessary and accessible means to protest and to disrupt the machinery of Oppression.

The United States has constrained our Black sons taken Captive in its Armies, to bear arms against their black, brown and yellow Brothers, to be the Executioners of these Friends and Brethren, or to fall themselves by their Hands.

The Exploitation and Injustice of the United States have incited domestic Insurrections [antigovernment uprisings] among us, and the United States has endeavored to bring on the Inhabitants of our ghettos, the merciless Military Establishment, whose known Rule of control is an undistinguished shooting of all Ages, Sexes and Conditions of Black People:

For being lynched, burned, tortured, harried, harassed and imprisoned without Just Cause.

For being gunned down in the streets, in our churches, in our homes, in our apartments and on our campuses, by Policemen and Troops who are protected by a mock Trial, from Punishment for any Murders which they commit on the Inhabitants of our Communities.

For creating, through Racism and bigotry, an unrelenting Economic Depression in the Black Community which wreaks havoc upon our men and disheartens our youth.

We will move to renounce all Allegiance to this Nation, and will refuse, in every way, to cooperate with the Evil which is Perpetrated upon ourselves and our Communities.

For denying to most of us equal access to the better Housing and Education of the land.

For having desecrated and torn down our humblest dwelling places, under the Pretense of Urban Renewal, without replacing them at costs which we can afford.

The United States has denied our personhood by refusing to teach our heritage, and the magnificent contributions to the life, wealth and growth of this Nation which have been made by Black People.

Government Has Ignored Polite Entreaties

In every stage of these Oppressions we have Petitioned for Redress in the most humble terms: Our repeated Petitions have been answered mainly by repeated Injury. A Nation, whose Character is thus marked by every act which may define a Racially Oppressive Regime, is unfit to receive the respect of a Free People.

Nor have we been wanting in attentions to our White Brethren. We have warned them from time to time of Attempts by their Structures of Power to extend an unwarranted, Repressive Control over us. We have reminded them of the Circumstances of our Captivity and Settlement here. We have appealed to their vaunted Justice and Magnanimity, and we have conjured them by the Ties of our Common Humanity to disavow these Injustices, which would inevitably interrupt our Connections and Correspondence. They have been deaf to the voice of Justice and of Humanity. We must, therefore, acquiesce [submit quietly] in the Necessity, which hereby announces our Most Firm Commitment to the Liberation of Black People, and hold the Institutions, Traditions and Systems of the United States as we hold the rest of the societies of Mankind, Enemies when Unjust and Tyrannical; when Just and Free, Friends.

We, therefore, the Black People of the United States of America, in all parts of this Nation, appealing to the Supreme Judge of the World for the Rectitude [moral correctness] of our Intentions, do, in the Name of our good People and our own Black Heroes—Richard Allen [former slave and church founder], James Varick [church leader], Absalom Jones [church founder], Nat Turner [led slave revolt], Frederick Douglas [antislavery intellectual], Marcus Garvey [founder of Universal Negro Improvement Association], Malcom X [leader of the Black Muslim movement], Martin Luther King, Jr. [civil rights leader] and all Black People past and present, great and small—Solemnly Publish and Declare, that we shall be, and of Right ought to be, FREE AND INDEPENDENT FROM THE INJUSTICE, EXPLOITATIVE CONTROL, INSTITUTIONALIZED VIOLENCE AND RACISM OF WHITE America, that unless we receive full Redress and Relief from these Inhumanities we will move to renounce all Allegiance to this Nation, and will refuse, in every way, to cooperate with the Evil which is Perpetrated upon ourselves and our Communities. And for the support of this Declaration, with a firm Reliance on the Protection of divine Providence, we mutually pledge to each other our Lives, our Fortunes, and our Sacred Honor.

Signed, by Order and in behalf of Black People,

NATIONAL COMMITTEE OF BLACK CHURCHMEN, INC.

New York Times, July 3, 1970

A Declaration of Interdependence Promotes Global Unity

Henry Steele Commager

Though its language and structure were modeled after the Declaration of Independence, the Declaration of Interdependence has an entirely different focus. Instead of touting America's rights to live independent of another country, this declaration acknowledges the interdependence and mutual responsibility the United States shares with other nations in preserving a peaceful and healthy world. This document was commissioned and published by the World Affairs Council of Philadelphia, a group of leaders and citizens interested in guiding America's foreign policy. Written by historian Henry Steele Commager, this Declaration of Interdependence was signed by members of Congress on July 4, 1976, the bicentennial of the signing of the original Declaration of Independence.

When in the course of history the threat of extinction confronts mankind, it is necessary for the people of The United States to declare their interdependence with the people of all nations and to embrace those principles and build those institutions which will enable mankind to survive and civilization to flourish.

Two centuries ago our forefathers brought forth a new nation; now we must join with others to bring forth a new world order. On this historic occasion it is proper that the American people should reaffirm those principles on which the United States of America was founded, acknowledge the new crises which confront them, accept the new obligations which history imposes upon them, and set forth the causes which impel them to affirm before all peoples their commitment to a Declaration of Interdependence.

People from All Nations Are Equal

We hold these truths to be self-evident: that all men are created equal; that the inequalities and injustices which afflict so much of the human race are the product of history and society, not of God or nature; that people everywhere are entitled to the blessings of life and liberty, peace and security and the realization of their full potential; that they have an inescapable moral obligation to preserve those rights for posterity; and that to achieve these ends all the peoples and nations of the globe should acknowledge their interdependence and join together to dedicate their minds and their hearts to the solution of those problems which threaten their survival.

To establish a new world order of compassion, peace, justice and security, it is essential that mankind free itself from the limitations of national prejudice, and acknowledge that the forces that unite it are incomparably deeper than those that divide it—that all people are part of one global community, dependent on one body of resources, bound together by the ties of a common humanity and associated in a common adventure on the planet Earth.

Let us then join together to vindicate and realize this great truth that mankind is one, and as one will nobly save or irreparably lose the heritage of thousands of years of civilization. And let us set forth the principles which should animate and inspire us if our civilization is to survive.

Nations Must Preserve and Share Earth's Resources

WE AFFIRM that the resources of the globe are finite, not infinite, that they are the heritage of no one nation or generation, but of all peoples, nations and of posterity, and that our deepest obligation is to transmit to that posterity a planet richer in material bounty, in beauty and in delight than we found it. Narrow notions of national sovereignty must not be permitted to curtail that obligation.

WE AFFIRM that the exploitation of the poor by the rich,

and the weak by the strong violates our common humanity and denies to large segments of society the blessings of life, liberty and happiness. We recognize a moral obligation to strive for a more prudent and more equitable sharing of the resources of the earth in order to ameliorate [lessen] poverty, hunger and disease.

WE AFFIRM that the resources of nature are sufficient to nourish and sustain all the present inhabitants of the globe and that there is an obligation on every society to distribute those resources equitably, along with a corollary [matching] obligation upon every society to assure that its population does not place upon Nature a burden heavier than it can bear.

What One Nation Does Affects All

WE AFFIRM our responsibility to help create conditions which will make for peace and security and to build more effective machinery for keeping peace among the nations. Because the insensate [senseless] accumulation of nuclear, chemical and biological weapons threatens the survival of Mankind we call for the immediate reduction and eventual elimination of these weapons under international supervision. We deplore the reliance on force to settle disputes between nation states and between rival groups within such states.

Let us then join together to vindicate and realize this great truth that mankind is one, and as one will nobly save or irreparably lose the heritage of thousands of years of civilization.

WE AFFIRM that the oceans are the common property of mankind whose dependence on their incomparable resources of nourishment and strength will, in the next century, become crucial for human survival, and that their exploitation should be so regulated as to serve the interests of the entire globe, and of future generations.

WE AFFIRM that pollution flows with the waters and flies with the winds, that it recognizes no boundary lines and penetrates all defenses, that it works irreparable damage alike to Nature and to Mankind—threatening with extinction the life of the seas, the flora and fauna of the earth, the health of the people in cities and the countryside alike—and that it can be adequately controlled only through international cooperation.

WE AFFIRM that the exploration and utilization of outer space is a matter equally important to all the nations of the globe and that no nation can be permitted to exploit or develop the potentialities of the planetary system exclusively for its own benefit.

WE AFFIRM that the economy of all nations is a seamless web, and that no one nation can any longer effectively maintain its processes of production and monetary systems without recognizing the necessity for collaborative regulation by international authorities.

WE AFFIRM that in a civilized society, the institutions of science and the arts are never at war and call upon all nations to exempt these institutions from the claims of chauvinistic [blind attachment to one's own group] nationalism and to foster that great community of learning and creativity whose benign function it is to advance civilization and the health and happiness of mankind.

WE AFFIRM that a world without law is a world without order, and we call upon all nations to strengthen and to sustain the United Nations and its specialized agencies, and other institutions of world order, and to broaden the jurisdiction of the World Court, that these may preside over a reign of law that will not only end wars but end as well that mindless violence which terrorizes our society even in times of peace.

The United States Must Cooperate with Other Nations

We can no longer afford to make little plans, allow ourselves to be the captives of events and forces over which we have no control, consult our fears rather than our hopes. We call upon the American people, on the threshold of the third century of their national existence, to display once again that boldness, enterprise, magnanimity [generosity] and vision which enabled the founders of our Republic to bring forth a new nation and inaugurate a new era in human history. The fate of humanity hangs in the balance. Throughout the globe, hearts and hopes wait upon us. We summon all Mankind to unite to meet the great challenge.

The Declaration Established a Worthy Goal

Marvin E. Frankel

As attorney and law professor Marvin E. Frankel points out, the Declaration of Independence and other documents like it have been open to criticism for their bold statements about the equality of all people. Frankel focuses his discussion on one of the harshest critics of the French Revolutionary Declaration of the Rights of Man and Citizen, Jeremy Bentham, an English philosopher who said that its language about equality and liberty not only were untrue in eighteenth-century France but would never be true in the country's future. Also a critic of America's Declaration of Independence, Bentham said that to call all a country's people equal and free when a large number of them were slaves was blatant hypocrisy. So the question remains: Should twenty-first-century citizens and leaders insist, as Bentham did, that such declarations be discredited because the countries for whom they were written do not live up to their lofty ideals? Frankel concludes that though America still has a long way to go in securing equal rights for many of its citizens, the call to do so remains a worthy goal that should guide public policy and law.

A little more than 200 years ago, [English philosopher] Jeremy Bentham turned his steely gaze on the French Revolutionary Declaration of the Rights of Man and Citizen. He found it a mess of sloppy ambiguities, illogic and smug foolishness. The least of his objections was that the French revolutionists were engaged in subversion, in "teaching grandmothers to suck eggs." But his denunciations ran mostly to greater ferocity. Where the Declaration spoke of "natural rights," he termed this simple nonsense; where it rose to describe "natural and imprescriptible rights," he called this "rhetorical nonsense—nonsense upon stilts."

Closely related to the pronouncement on "natural rights" was the proclamation that "men are born and remain free, and equal in respect of rights." The revolutionists declared liberty and equality as describing "natural" qualities "prior to the existence of government" and not dependent, therefore, on government creation, support or enforcement.

"All men born free?" Bentham asked sardonically. How could anyone say this at a time when "so many men [were] born slaves"? Equal? "The right of the heir of the most indigent [poor] family equal to the rights of the heir of the most wealthy?" He went on to a list of contrasts. We could all add to it today: Michael Jordan versus the veriest klutz, Einstein as opposed to an idiot, the genetically joyous and those of us who come woebegone from the womb.

The Language About Equality Was an Ideal

Bentham's barbs could be turned no less aptly against our own, earlier Declaration of Independence. When Thomas Jefferson wrote that all were created equal, did he just happen to overlook the scores of slaves in his household, including at least one who could scarcely choose as an equal whether to gratify his lust? There is no way to doubt that the august signers of our Declaration knew as well as we do about the stark inequalities among humans—in endowments, social distinctions, inherited wealth, and all the other chance delights or miseries with which fate visits us.

Even Jefferson, for all his tawdry rationalizations on the subject, knew that his slaves were in no remote sense allowed to be "equal" to other folks. So the Declaration of Independence, grand as it is in many respects, is tarnished by an overcast of hypocrisy, blind assumptions about the world of its authors, and prematurely Orwellian doublethink [simultaneous belief in two contradictory ideas].

In its first sentence, our Declaration invoked "the Laws of Nature and of Nature's God" to justify the break from Britain. The issue raised by these references to "natural law" remains a lively one to this day. I share Bentham's skeptical view of the idea that the Creator fashioned these "natural rights." The notion of "natural law" generally, at least in the simple formulation of the Declarations and other 18th-century expressions, offers anything but a recipe for clear thinking.

Jeremy Bentham

As described by Jefferson and others, natural law was part of the "Laws of Nature," like Sir Isaac Newton's law of gravity and Robert Boyle's law regarding the behavior of gases. In this sense the idea is fatuous [silly]. So far as we know, when we speak of Boyle's and Newton's "laws" we mean regularities that humans were able to perceive but whose existence they were in no way responsible for. If or when somebody heats a gas and it contracts, we will have to revisit and possibly revise Boyle's "law."

The right to due process [consistent legal procedures], on the other hand, however much we cherish it, is a human creation (and a recent one at that) subject to human revision or repeal. The confusion between observed and enacted law has led over the centuries to an acceptance of doctrines ranging from the right to own slaves to the rights of workers and their bosses to contract for an 80-hour week. We have survived such things, but other inanities continue to be trumpeted as matters of natural law, often as excuses for assaults on individual freedom.

Bentham expressed his own conclusions in stark jeremiads [complaints]. He observed that on "the subject of the fundamental principles of government, we have seen what execrable trash the choicest talents of the French nation have produced." Contrasting the world's admiration for France's contributions to the understanding of chemistry, he found the Declaration of Rights not only foolish but dangerous. He condemned the "imaginary laws" proposed by any declaration of rights. He saw all such declarations as "the mortal enemies of law, the subverters of government, and the assassins of security."

The Declaration Describes What Ought to Be

If the charges in Bentham's indictment stand, what are we to conclude at the millennium? Despite the soundness of his position that both the French and the American Declarations were "inaccurate" when they said "all men are created equal," time has refuted his view that those pronouncements were nonsense, with or without stilts. In the verdict of history, the key is the important distinction between what is and what ought to be.

Tinctured perhaps with hypocrisy and with some convenient ambiguity in its inception, our Declaration is best seen as the statement of an ideal, unfolding still and still to be realized more fully. It required almost a hundred years and a ghastly Civil War before the Fourteenth Amendment undertook, with a special eye to the freed slaves, to guarantee for everyone "the equal protection of the laws." That too was an aspiration, a promise not yet kept more than partially. With detours and sporadic backsliding, we continue on the journey to achieve this ideal.

Even Jefferson, for all his tawdry rationalizations on the subject, knew that his slaves were in no remote sense allowed to be "equal" to other folks.

Even as an aspiration, the declaration of equality in 1776 was too narrowly shared in a slaveholding society to shine as the universal beacon the signers may have thought themselves to have lighted. Today, in courthouses and on the streets, aspects of the full meaning of equal rights as a goal remain contentious. But we know now, perhaps better than Bentham did, the force of shared aspirations, firmly asserted in a society that strives to be democratic—and scarcely anyone doubts that the statement and evolution of the ideal have moved the species toward a higher plane.

Far from being junked as Bentham's scorn would have dictated, the idea of equal rights has spread around the world. . . . December 10 [1998] marked the 50th anniversary of the Universal Declaration of Human Rights, drafted by the United Nations Human Rights Commission with Eleanor Roosevelt as Chair. Its seventh Article, in phrases long familiar to Americans, says:

> All are equal before the law and are entitled without any discrimination to equal protection of the law. All are entitled to equal protection against any discrimination in violation of this Declaration and against any incitement to such discrimination.

America Has Far to Go Toward Securing Rights for All

As the oldest contemporary democracy steadily in business, we have a right to take pride in our two centuries of moral and political leadership toward the Universal Declaration. At the same time, we should note some arguable evidence that we have been slipping from our place in the front ranks of the ongoing struggle for equal rights. The United States has lagged behind many countries—France, England, even Russia—in ratifying an array of more recent human rights covenants.

Our celebration of ourselves, clearly, should be tempered by the knowledge that we have a long way to go.

An incomplete list of the commitments we have thus far failed to formally accept includes those on Economic, Social and Cultural Rights; on the Rights of the Child; and on the Elimination of All Forms of Discrimination Against Women. Then there is our enthusiastic and increasing use of the death penalty, at a point when it has effectively been abolished in all the democracies of the West. That is a serious lapse when you consider the poor, the deprived, and the minority origins of almost all death row inhabitants.

Our celebration of ourselves, clearly, should be tempered by the knowledge that we have a long way to go. A recent book by a great legal scholar casts light on the path to be taken. Professor Charles L. Black Jr., who has inspired law students at Columbia and Yale for over half a century, sets forth eloquently in *A New Birth of Freedom* (1997) his thesis that the Declaration of Independence, far from being simply an ancient icon, should serve as a steadily fresh and generative "commitment," with "the force of law," to the securing of vital and as yet unrealized blessings. The sort of thing he has in mind ranges from the erasure of poverty ("a constitutional justice of livelihood") to a true protection for sexual preference and individual lifestyles generally.

Black challenges the judges, the lawmakers, and all of us to see that the Declaration's "right to the pursuit of happiness" should entail steady extensions of "human rights, named and unnamed." His is a dramatic step beyond Bentham's solid but dry and incomplete logic. If the Declaration did not describe accurately conditions then current, it did prescribe an unlimited vista of human possibilities. Black recognizes that the winds of legal history have blown recurrently in the face of his vision. But he continues in his ninth decade to keep it brightly in view. So should we all.

Appendix: The Declaration of Independence

The Declaration of Independence of the Thirteen Colonies
In CONGRESS, July 4, 1776

The unanimous Declaration of the thirteen united States of America,

When in the Course of human events, it becomes necessary for one people to dissolve the political bands which have connected them with another, and to assume among the powers of the earth, the separate and equal station to which the Laws of Nature and of Nature's God entitle them, a decent respect to the opinions of mankind requires that they should declare the causes which impel them to the separation.

We hold these truths to be self-evident, that all men are created equal, that they are endowed by their Creator with certain unalienable Rights, that among these are Life, Liberty and the pursuit of Happiness.—That to secure these rights, Governments are instituted among Men, deriving their just powers from the consent of the governed,—That whenever any Form of Government becomes destructive of these ends, it is the Right of the People to alter or to abolish it, and to institute new Government, laying its foundation on such principles and organizing its powers in such form, as to them shall seem most likely to effect their Safety and Happiness. Prudence, indeed, will dictate that Governments long established should not be changed for light and transient causes; and accordingly all experience hath shewn, that mankind are more disposed to suffer, while evils are sufferable, than to right themselves by abolishing the forms to which they are accustomed. But when a long train of abuses and usurpations, pursuing invariably the same Object evinces a design to reduce them under absolute Despotism, it is their right, it is their duty, to throw off such Government, and to provide new Guards for their future security.—Such has been the patient sufferance of these Colonies; and such is now the necessity which constrains them to alter their former Systems of Government. The history of the present King of Great Britain [George III] is a history of repeated injuries and usurpations, all having in direct object the establishment of an absolute Tyranny over these States. To prove this, let Facts be submitted to a candid world.

He has refused his Assent to Laws, the most wholesome and necessary for the public good.

He has forbidden his Governors to pass Laws of immediate and pressing importance, unless suspended in their operation till his Assent should be obtained; and when so suspended, he has utterly neglected to attend to them.

He has refused to pass other Laws for the accommodation of large districts of people, unless those people would relinquish the right of Representation in the Legislature, a right inestimable to them and formidable to tyrants only.

He has called together legislative bodies at places unusual, uncomfortable, and distant from the depository of their public Records, for the sole purpose of fatiguing them into compliance with his measures.

He has dissolved Representative Houses repeatedly, for opposing with manly firmness his invasions on the rights of the people.

He has refused for a long time, after such dissolutions, to cause others to be elected; whereby the Legislative powers, incapable of Annihilation, have returned to the People at large for their exercise; the State remaining in the mean time exposed to all the dangers of invasion from without, and convulsions within.

He has endeavoured to prevent the population of these States; for that purpose obstructing the Laws for Naturalization of Foreigners; refusing to pass others to encourage their migrations hither, and raising the conditions of new Appropriations of Lands.

He has obstructed the Administration of Justice, by refusing his Assent to Laws for establishing Judiciary powers.

He has made Judges dependent on his Will alone, for the tenure of their offices, and the amount and payment of their salaries.

He has erected a multitude of New Offices, and sent hither swarms of Officers to harass our people, and eat out their substance.

He has kept among us, in times of peace, Standing Armies without the consent of our legislatures.

He has affected to render the Military independent of and superior to the Civil power.

He has combined with others to subject us to a jurisdiction foreign to our constitution and unacknowledged by our laws; giving his Assent to their Acts of pretended Legislation:

For Quartering large bodies of armed troops among us:

For protecting them, by a mock Trial, from punishment for any Murders which they should commit on the Inhabitants of these States:

For cutting off our Trade with all parts of the world:

For imposing Taxes on us without our Consent:

For depriving us, in many cases, of the benefits of Trial by Jury:

For transporting us beyond Seas to be tried for pretended offences:

For abolishing the free System of English Laws in a neighbouring Province, establishing therein an Arbitrary government, and enlarging its Boundaries so as to render it at once an example and fit instrument for introducing the same absolute rule into these Colonies:

For taking away our Charters, abolishing our most valuable Laws, and altering fundamentally the Forms of our Governments:

For suspending our own Legislatures, and declaring themselves invested with power to legislate for us in all cases whatsoever.

He has abdicated Government here, by declaring us out of his Protection and waging War against us.

He has plundered our seas, ravaged our Coasts, burnt our towns, and destroyed the lives of our people.

He is at this time transporting large Armies of foreign Mercenaries to compleat the works of death, desolation and tyranny, already begun with circumstances of Cruelty and perfidy scarcely paralleled in the most barbarous ages, and totally unworthy the Head of a civilized nation.

He has constrained our fellow Citizens taken Captive on the high Seas to bear Arms against their Country, to become the executioners of their friends and Brethren, or to fall themselves by their Hands.

He has excited domestic insurrections amongst us, and has endeavoured to bring on the inhabitants of our frontiers, the merciless Indian Savages, whose known rule of warfare, is an undistinguished destruction of all ages, sexes and conditions.

In every stage of these Oppressions We have Petitioned for Redress in the most humble terms: Our repeated Petitions have been answered only by repeated injury. A Prince whose character is thus marked by every act which may define a Tyrant, is unfit to be the ruler of a free people.

Nor have We been wanting in attentions to our British brethren. We have warned them from time to time of attempts by their legislature to extend an unwarrantable jurisdiction over us. We have reminded them of the circumstances of our emigration and settlement here. We have appealed to their native justice and magnanimity, and we have conjured them by the ties of our common kindred to disavow these usurpations, which, would inevitably interrupt our connections and correspondence. They too have been deaf to the voice of justice and of consanguinity. We must, therefore, acquiesce in the necessity, which denounces our Separation, and hold them, as we hold the rest of mankind, Enemies in War, in Peace Friends.

We, therefore, the Representatives of the united States of America, in General Congress, Assembled, appealing to the Supreme Judge of the world for the rectitude of our intentions, do, in the Name, and by the Authority of the good People of these Colonies, solemnly publish and declare, That these United Colonies are, and of Right ought to be Free and Independent States; that they are Absolved from all Allegiance to the British Crown, and that all political connection between them and the State of Great Britain, is and ought to be totally dissolved; and that as Free and Independent States, they have full Power to levy War, conclude Peace, contract Alliances, establish Commerce, and to do all other Acts and Things which Independent States may of right do. And for the support of this Declaration, with a firm reliance on the protection of divine Providence, we mutually pledge to each other our Lives, our Fortunes and our sacred Honor.

For Further Research

Carl Becker, *The Declaration of Independence: A Study in the History of Political Ideas.* New York: Vintage Books, 1970.

Silvio A. Bedini, *The Declaration of Independence Desk: Relic of Revolution.* Washington, DC: Smithsonian Institution Press, 1981.

Jim Bishop, *Birth of the United States.* New York: Morrow, 1976.

Julian Boyd, *The Declaration of Independence: The Evolution of the Texts as Shown in Facsimiles of Various Drafts by Its Author, Thomas Jefferson.* Princeton, NJ: Princeton University Press, 1945.

Andrew Burstein, *America's Jubilee: How in 1826 a Generation Remembered Fifty Years of Independence.* New York: Knopf, 2001.

Harold K. Bush Jr., *American Declarations.* Urbana: University of Illinois Press, 1999.

Donald Cooke, *Our Nation's Great Heritage.* Maplewood, NJ: Hammond, 1972.

Alonzo Thomas Dill, *Carter Braxton, Virginia Signer.* Lanham, MD: University Press of America, 1983.

T.R. Fehrenbach, *Greatness to Spare: The Heroic Sacrifices of the Men Who Signed the Declaration of Independence.* Princeton, NJ: D. Van Nostrand, 1968.

Bruce Allyn Findlay and Esther Blair Findlay, *Your Magnificent Declaration.* New York: Holt, Rinehart & Winston, 1961.

Sam Fink, *The Fifty-Six Who Signed.* New York: McCall, 1971.

Jay Fliegelman, *Declaring Independence: Jefferson, Natural Language, and the Culture of Performance.* Stanford, CA: Stanford University Press, 1993.

Russell Freedman, *Give Me Liberty: Story of the Declaration of Independence.* New York: Holiday House, 2000.

David Freeman Hawke, *Honorable Treason: The Declaration of Independence and the Men Who Signed It*. New York: Viking, 1976.

John Hazelton, *The Declaration of Independence: Its History*. New York: Da Capo Press, 1970.

Allen Jayne, *Jefferson's Declaration of Independence: Origins, Philosophy, and Theology*. Lexington: University Press of Kentucky, 1998.

Cornell Lengyel, *Four Days in July: The Story Behind the Declaration of Independence*. Garden City, NY: Doubleday, 1958.

Tibor Machan, ed., *Individual Rights Considered: Are the Truths of the U.S. Declaration of Independence Lasting?* Stanford, CA: Hoover Institution, 2001.

Dumas Malone, *Story of the Declaration of Independence*. New York: Oxford University Press, 1954.

John Chester Miller, *Wolf by the Ears: Thomas Jefferson and Slavery*. New York: Free Press, 1977.

Edmund S. Morgan, *The Meaning of Independence*. Charlottesville: University Press of Virginia, 1976.

Index